To Danny
I Love You Much
Rhonda Anderson

Kingdom Intercession

A Powerful Gift from God

A Deeper Love

RHONDA ANDERSON

WESTBOW
PRESS
A DIVISION OF THOMAS NELSON
& ZONDERVAN

Copyright © 2014 Rhonda Anderson.

All rights reserved. No part of this book may be used or reproduced by any means, graphic, electronic, or mechanical, including photocopying, recording, taping or by any information storage retrieval system without the written permission of the publisher except in the case of brief quotations embodied in critical articles and reviews.

Scripture taken from the King James Version of the Bible.
Scriptures taken from the Holy Bible, New International Version®, NIV®. Copyright © 1973, 1978, 1984, 2011 by Biblica, Inc.™ Used by permission of Zondervan. All rights reserved worldwide. www.zondervan.com The "NIV" and "New International Version" are trademarks registered in the United States Patent and Trademark Office by Biblica, Inc.™ All rights reserved.

Word definitions by Merriam-Webster, *Merriam-Webster's Collegiate Dictionary*, Eleventh Edition, principal copyright 2003.

Word definitions indicated by *The Prophets Dictionary*, Paula Price, *The Prophet's Dictionary*, Revised and Expanded Edition (New Kensington, PA: Whitaker House, 2006).

WestBow Press books may be ordered through booksellers or by contacting:

WestBow Press
A Division of Thomas Nelson & Zondervan
1663 Liberty Drive
Bloomington, IN 47403
www.westbowpress.com
1 (866) 928-1240

Because of the dynamic nature of the Internet, any web addresses or links contained in this book may have changed since publication and may no longer be valid. The views expressed in this work are solely those of the author and do not necessarily reflect the views of the publisher, and the publisher hereby disclaims any responsibility for them.

Book cover design: Kristine Cotterman, © Exodus Design Studios. Used by permission.

ISBN: 978-1-4908-4379-7 (sc)
ISBN: 978-1-4908-4380-3 (hc)
ISBN: 978-1-4908-4429-9 (e)

Library of Congress Control Number: 2014912159

Printed in the United States of America.

WestBow Press rev. date: 08/20/2014

CONTENTS

Acknowledgments ix

Introduction xi

Chapter 1   The Message 1

Chapter 2   The Passion of Prayer 5

Chapter 3   The Prayer Vessel 17

Chapter 4   Spiritual Vision 27

Chapter 5   Praying the Divine Target 39

Chapter 6   Holy Communion 63

Chapter 7   From the Heart of an Intercessor 73

Connect with the Author 95

To every human spirit seeking change in their lives
To the intercessors and prayer warriors on the wall
To the churches for the work of the ministry
To my beloved family for your love and support
To the future generations as a seed to sow
Most of all, to my heavenly Father to use for his glory

And all things, whatsoever ye shall ask in
prayer, believing, ye shall receive.
—Matthew 21:22

ACKNOWLEDGMENTS

To my beloved parents, Roland and Carol Anderson. Thank you for always encouraging me to press forward. You have poured into my life and assisted in my training and development in my spiritual walk in Christ. Thank you for allowing God to use you to equip me. I am forever grateful.

To Apostle Steve Foreman, a great leader and pastor. Thank you for your intense teaching of the Scriptures and how to search out the Word of God. Your impartations and methodology for feasting on the Scriptures have added to my life and prepared me for the work God has for me.

To Bishop Melvin Williams, a spiritual father forever. Thank you for giving me the foundation I needed in my spiritual walk. You taught me many things, but most of all how to pray, worship, and sow into the lives of others. You are truly a gift from God.

INTRODUCTION

Kingdom Intercession identifies prayer as one of the most powerful gifts God has given to humanity. Prayer helps us to build our relationships with God as we communicate with him. Intercession promotes opportunity for God to respond when we intercede for others, nations, or the continents of the world.

This book is a collection of inspired writing to assist in developing a strong and more effective prayer life. Each segment provides insight to different areas of prayer that will enhance your relationship with God as the Holy Spirit draws you closer to him. You will also find that the Word of God is the cornerstone of prayer. Throughout the collection are Scriptures that support the authenticity of praying. The topics have been tailored to walk you through an increasingly prayerful journey as the relationship between you and your Father in heaven grows.

This assemblage has seven main objectives:

1. Learn and understand that you are the vessel God uses when you pray.
2. Discover a love and passion for prayer.
3. Feed your necessity for spiritual insight.
4. Gain knowledge on how praying the target produces results.

5. Learn how applying God's Word in your prayer dialogue generates effective prayers.
6. Recognize the urgency for intercession.
7. Understand how prayer and intercession plow the soil so the "Kingdom of God" message can be preached to the entire world.

Kingdom intercession is not an isolated teaching but rather an integrated prayer method that builds a strong and more effective prayer life by applying biblical beliefs and knowledge to which we all have access.

In our current hour, there is urgency for prayer and intercession. Both should be an essential part of our daily lives. Can you imagine how this world would be if everyone prayed to God without ceasing? Our existence here on earth would be transformed forever. Faith is the power behind prayer. Prayer and faith have the same characteristics; they are the substance of things unseen, and they both have power beyond things that are seen. When we pray, we must remember that prayer is more than just words; it is words with power.

CHAPTER 1

The Message

Kingdom intercession is an inspired message, an urgent call intended for anyone who has ears to hear the call to prayer. Its aim is to encourage God's people to spend more time in prayer, interceding on behalf of others. The overall goal is for God's will to be done in the lives of his people. There is a great and increasing need for intercession as a key instrument for communicating with our Father in heaven so his will may be manifested on earth. Many people pray, but there are not many who intercede for others.

Intercession is unique because it moves from individual focus to a shared center of attention. Intercession causes our prayers to stretch beyond our parameters to include others. Going beyond the inner core of our own personal desires allows us to tap into what God desires. Jesus knew his assignment on earth was to save God's people. Our Father in heaven is not only concerned about the individual but also the multitude of people. God works in the multitude. Look at it this way. You can pick up one leaf at a time or you can use a rake to gather many leaves. This is what kingdom intercession does on a spiritual level, for the kingdom of God is not just for one person but also for the collective of people.

Throughout the Scriptures, the kingdom is expressed not only from a geographical point of view but also from a spiritual perspective. Matthew 6:33 tells us, "But seek ye first the kingdom of God, and his righteousness; and all these things shall be added unto you." This Scripture informs us that things are added when we seek his kingdom and his righteousness. Seeking the kingdom of God should be our approach to and road map for everything we do in life.

Kingdom intercession means proactively seeking our Father in heaven with all our hearts, minds, and souls to intercede on behalf of the people, governments, nations, and continents of this world. The need for intercession can be for various reasons, circumstances, and situations, but the supporting foundation should be praying for the will of God.

Our Father in heaven is patient with us, not wanting anyone to perish, but time is of the essence. Today, the demand for prayer is stronger than ever. For far too long, prayer has been purposely overlooked and taken very lightly and with vast limitations. Every believer should have a prayer life, for the word *believer* is more than just a label. It means one who believes wholeheartedly in the Word of God. A true believer cannot pick and choose certain parts of the Word to believe and apply them. To believe is to believe all of it. In 1 Thessalonians 5:17, we are told to "pray without ceasing." God has graciously given all of us a great privilege and honor called prayer, which allows us access to him at any time. It is a gift from God that exhibits our ultimate relationship with him, a gift that can never be replicated by mankind.

Prayer allows us to commune with our Father in heaven. The Scriptures tell us in Genesis 1:26 that God made us in his image.

That image has made us unique because of our likeness to God. This is not new information, but it is how we begin to understand the accessibility we have to the Father. We can access him because we have a relational connection that was established in the creation of man.

Believers today have access to God. Accessibility means "capable of being reached."[1] We are able to reach God through prayer and intercession. This is an awesome privilege and should not be taken for granted. Even the world has controls in place for accessibility to prominent people such as kings, queens, presidents, etc., and without special permission, access is denied. Nevertheless, we have direct access anytime we desire to reach the King of all kings, the Creator of heaven and earth. The keys to that direct access are prayer and intercession.

Although prayer is a spiritual exercise, many still do not understand its true significance and power. The true power of prayer is beyond human reasoning; carnal thinking could never comprehend the magnitude of prayer. The power of prayer has been misunderstood and at times distorted from its true purpose. Some treat prayer as a last choice, whereas it should be the first. For believers, prayer should be the first responder. In most cases, we wait until something happens before praying versus praying *before* something happens. Yet there are many cases in the Scriptures that are testimonies of fervent prayer changing destiny. One of my favorite biblical reminders is in Genesis 18 when Abraham prayed for Lot before the destruction of Sodom. These testimonies help us understand the impact of prayer.

Kingdom intercession is designed to teach us to pray and rediscover the purpose of our relationships with God through prayer.

---

[1] *Merriam-Webster's Collegiate Dictionary.* Springfield, Massachusetts, U.S.A.: Merriam-Webster, Incorporated, 2012.

The function of the message is to invoke prayer in the lives of God's people into another dimension. Until we can understand what God has placed inside all of us and how valuable this is, we will not understand the purpose of prayer. There is a pressing call to prayer from a kingdom perspective for intercession to the whole world. Souls are being lost, and people are dying daily without the full knowledge of God and the opportunity of salvation. True intercession and intimate prayers are needed now for the multitude.

As a prophetic intercessor with a great passion for prayer, it is my hope and prayer that God's kingdom messages will reach the whole world in the name of Jesus.

> And it came to pass, that, as he was praying in a certain place, when he ceased, one of his disciples said unto him, Lord, teach us to pray, as John also taught his disciples. And he said unto them, when ye pray, say, Our Father which art in heaven, Hallowed be thy name. Thy Kingdom come. Thy will be done, as in heaven, so in earth.
>
> —Luke 11:1–2 (KJV)

CHAPTER 2

The Passion of Prayer

The passion of prayer begins with our passions for God. When we have a zeal for God, our desires to pray becomes an exciting part of our love relationships with him. I describe passion as something planted deep within your heart that brings forth a strong sense of excitement whenever you engage in it. Having a passion for prayer is like falling in love with the only one in the world who truly loves you and understands who you are. Prayer is the inner core of your relationship with God, and everyone has the option to activate this privilege.

Praying is not a preset formula of words but an outpouring of heartfelt expressions from your spirit. Prayer creates a love relationship with God that cannot be compared with any relationship you may have in life. It is a matter of respect, honor, adoration, and worship. If you have not discovered the total passion for prayer and intercession, perhaps you should reevaluate how much you truly know about the true and living God who has an eternal, undying, and never-ending love for you. Can you imagine a love so wonderful that it can never die? John 3:16 describes this love for us. God gave his son because he loved us so much. This describes the depth of his love; a love that has no boundaries. It is beyond measure and is not contained in an earthly capacity.

When you have a passion for prayer, you will sacrifice your time, sleep, and schedule to pray, not for a specified week or month, for prayer will be your lifestyle. You will become so comfortable in prayer that God will place something in your heart, and you will be prompted to pray on demand.

Anna the prophetess (Luke 2:37) served God with fasting and prayers night and day. To pray night and day is a true sign that a passion for prayer exists. I do not believe that everyone will have a passion for prayer, but I do believe that if you have a desire for the passion, God will give it to you. In the case of Anna the prophetess, I can only imagine what some people were saying about her praying night and day. Probably things like "She is always in the temple praying. Does she do anything else?" "Anna the widow should be home at night." "Must she pray all the time?" We must remember that carnal-minded people will not understand your passion for God when they do not have one.

> And there was one Anna, a prophetess, the daughter of Phanuel, of the tribe of Aser: she was of a great age, and had lived with an husband seven years from her virginity; And she was a widow of about fourscore and four years, which departed not from the temple, but served God with fastings and prayers night and day.
> —Luke 2:36–37

There are many who work at a job day and night because they want something in return—pay. Well, when we pray, we are also asking God for a return. The difference is that in a passion for prayer, you want what God wants on the return. You are more concerned about the will of God.

Prayer between you and God is all about transparency. Is there anything in you that God is not aware of? Even if there are things within that are not pleasing to him, he still loves you. A love relationship with God through prayer allows you to have an ear to his heart. When we can hear the heart of God in the spirit, we are transformed to want what he wants. Our desires become his desire. We surrender what we want to what he wants for us. This becomes a part of praying that his will be done on earth as it is in heaven.

Although God is a spirit and not a physical being, the love and compassion I have personally experienced through my relationship with him is far greater than any other relationship I have ever experienced. Through consistent prayer, love and passion grow deeply with God. The more you pray and spend time in his Word, the more likely it is that these things will happen:

- The more you pray, the more the relationship grows.
- The more you pray, the more you love God.
- The more you pray, the more you understand the will of God.
- The more you pray, the more you intercede for others.
- The more you pray, the more you see spiritually.
- The more you pray, the more you have visions and dreams.
- The more you pray, the more you understand your purpose in life.
- The more you pray, the more you can war in the spirit.
- The more you pray, the more you will repent.
- The more you pray, the more God will reveal spiritual matters.
- The more you pray, the more God will trust you.
- The more you pray, the more God will use you.

- The more you pray, the more peace you gain in your mind and spirit.
- The more you pray, the more you are able to stand in adversity.
- The more you pray, the more the image of God is reflected within you.
- The more you pray, the more you want to study and learn of God.
- The more you pray, the more time you will want to spend with God.
- The more you pray, the more wisdom you have.
- The more you pray, the more kingdom-minded you become.
- The more you pray, the more God will answer.

The list above is not a complete list because God is still moving and transforming us when we pray. The "more" represents the continuing factor that will be ever increasing because we never arrive at the end. Nevertheless, we are to strive to perfection in him and through him.

Prayer builds our relationships with God. This bond is unique and intimate, and its core is love. I have children and loved ones, and my love for them is built on different types of relationships. Having an understanding of the Holy Trinity helps describe relationships. God the Father, the Son, and the Holy Spirit all have the same Spirit but different relationships and functions. But they are all built on love, truth, and giving.

One day in my prayer time, I asked God to help me communicate to others how Jesus and the Holy Ghost are one with God in a simplified fashion. The Holy Spirit of God revealed this scenario to me: Rhonda is a daughter, mother, and grandmother, making me three-in-one. Although I am one person (in spirit), I have different love relationships and functions with all three. The relationship I have with my mother as her daughter is very different from the relationship I have with my children as their mother. Then on the other hand, the relationships I have with my grandchildren are totally different from the ones I have with my mother and my children.

God reveals himself to us in these forms: As the Father, he loves, provides, and cares for us. Through the Son of God, we know and understand the very nature and personality of God. Through the Holy Spirit, we know and understand the spiritual things of God. This brought a real-life understanding to the fullness of God and our relationships with him. And this is only one of many revelations birthed to me in prayer.

> For as the body is one, and hath many members, and all the members of that one body, being many, are one body: so also is Christ.
> —1 Corinthians 12:12

> I and my Father are one.
> —John 10:30

In consistent prayer, my passion deepens for the things of God. I may address God as my Father, especially when expressing his greatness and prominence in an attitude of thanksgiving. Other times, I may address the Holy Spirit for guidance, truth, and the power to sustain. There are also times when I may address the Son mostly for the nature of God, the kingdom, and during spiritual warfare. All three have significant meanings, especially in our prayer lives. Here are some examples of passionate expressions to each one:

My Father

My Father in heaven, you are not far away. You live within me. I love and adore you for who you are. My heart is filled with adoration and love for you. Your love stretches deep within the core of my soul, piercing my heart, causing me to seek you more and more. I glorify your name, great Jehovah. I lie before you, seeking your face, presence, and holiness. Words only touch the surface of your true identity. Your depth has no boundaries and reaches far beyond the spheres of this world. You are worthy to be praised at all times.

Father, I reverence you for who you are; the great I Am, the creator of heaven and earth. Thank you for loving, caring, and nurturing me despite my shortcomings. Only my Father in heaven can love me the way you do. I trust you because you are all-knowing, all-seeing, and all-wise. You are mighty and stronger than anything imaginable, and I bow down to you and worship you only.

Father, forgive me for every trespass I have committed against you and my brother in any form or fashion. I thank you for every provision you have made for me. You have equipped me with everything I need to please and glorify you. You formed me in my mother's womb and spoke me into existence with the breath of your Spirit. You have ordained my life and ordered my steps, and I give you glory. I lay down every burden to you because you are my Father in heaven, the one who takes care of all my needs. Please continue to transform and build me up to be used by you.

Father, I latch onto your hand as you draw me closer to you. Every morning is new with you, and every day is filled with your glory, unspeakable glory, unmeasured glory that shines brighter than any comparable light. If only the world could comprehend the light and true love of the Father. You created me with love everlasting, and I am your child created in your image to serve you. Continue to protect and shield me from the Enemy of this world. In you, there is safety and security with assurance of a place of rest that the world could never offer.

Father, there is none like you. Daniel called you the Ancient of Days; Jeremiah called you Lord of Righteousness; Ezekiel called you Sovereign; and David called you My Shepherd. Father, you are the God of Abraham, Isaac, Jacob, and the Gentiles. I am so overjoyed and thankful that you are still the same today and change not. I call you righteous, holy, and undefiled. Sovereignty is your nature, loving is your ways, and your statutes and commands govern my success in life.

Father, it is my prayer that the world comes into the full knowledge and understanding that you are the beginning and the end, the Alpha and Omega, the author and finisher of our faith. I pray that they no longer be blinded by the deception of the Enemy. I am so grateful that your kingdom is not of this world. I humbly give thanks to you for my daily bread, physical and spiritual. My gratitude is great for your divine purpose and plan for my life. Father, I am lifeless without you. My heart is beating because of you, and I can breathe the breath of life because of you. I exist because of you. Thank you.

The Son

Jesus, you are the Son of God, the Savior, and I love you. Thank you for being the ultimate sacrifice. Thank you for dying for my sins. Through the shedding of your blood, I can be forgiven. The prophet Isaiah calls you Prince of Peace, Mighty God, Everlasting Father, and Wonderful Counselor. God has highly exalted you and given you a name that is above every name according to Philippians 2:9.

You demonstrated the works of the Father here on earth so we could believe and understand the very nature of God himself. Thank you for being God's living example.

Jesus, you knew no sin. You are holy, innocent, undefiled, and unblemished. You are the perfect image of God in the flesh. John 1 proclaims, "In the beginning was the Word, and the Word was with God, and the Word was God. And then the Word was made flesh, and dwelt among us, full of grace and truth." Thank you for being the Word and becoming flesh so God's people would know who you are. Thank you for being wounded for our transgressions and bruised for our iniquities. By your stripes we are healed!

Jesus, you are the perfect example: teacher, prophet, evangelist, pastor, and apostle. Because of your teaching and exposition, witnesses were able to record your actions so the revelation of your coming would be known to all of us. Thank you, Jesus!

The anointing on your life brought prophecy to pass and is still bringing it to pass today. We can walk in the evangelistic calling today because you came to this earth and released the Great Commission to preach the kingdom of God to the entire world. The Word of God calls you the Good Shepherd in John 10:11 and tells us that the good shepherd gives his life for his sheep. You are the shepherd at the door, and the door is the way to the kingdom of God. Jesus, you are the Christ and the open door to everlasting life. Jesus, I pray that all shepherds and pastors receive the same anointing and have the same compassion you have for the sheep. You are the great apostle of all times. A great leader and mentor for the kingdom of God. You are complete, true, and authentic. I thank God for you!

Jesus, you have paved the way so we could be restored to our rightful positions on this earth. Thank you for the keys to the kingdom of God. Through revelation, you have given us the authority to bind and loose Satan and his activities here on earth, as it has already been done in heaven. In operation with the Holy Spirit, we can decree and declare, open and shut things on the earth, as we read in Matthew 18:18. Through your death, the veil has been torn and we have direct access to the Father in heaven. We can communicate with him directly because we are now and forever a royal priesthood through you, and most of all, our authority and dominion on this earth has been restored. Thank you, Jesus!

Jesus, thank you for being the perfect prayer vessel and model on how we should pray. The passion you revealed to the disciples regarding prayer set the standard for accessing the Father. The passion you made known to us concerning prayer is forever grateful. You are the example of what our positions should be in prayer when we approach the Father. In the garden of Gethsemane, you demonstrated your deep trust in God as you cried out to the Father in prayer. Your soul was exceedingly sorrowful, yet you prayed to the Father with humble and heartfelt sincerity. This shows us how deep our love should be for God. Jesus, thank you for instructing us how to pray and how not to pray in the Scriptures. In Matthew 6:5, you tell us not to pray as hypocrites but to enter into the secret place that is the very presence of God and commune with him in prayer. Thank you for being our example.

Holy Spirit

Good morning, Holy Spirit. I welcome you into my day. Lead me and guide me into all truth. Let your spirit overtake me, and let your voice override my voice. Fill me with your power, and enhance my spiritual capacity. I boldly confess that you are the Holy Spirit of God.

Holy Spirit, comfort me in my times of trouble so the peace of God may be upon me. Let your consoling spirit strengthen me. Relieve any distress from the course of my day and throughout the night hour. As the wiles of this world try to approach my dwelling, let your spirit of discernment quickly identify them and disarm the Enemy's tactics. Go before me and make the crooked paths straight.

Holy Spirit, teach me spiritual things concerning the Father. I gladly receive your instructions and guidance. Enhance my prayer life as you teach me to pray with a kingdom mind-set. Search my heart and stir the spirit within me as intercession is made with the Father through you.

Holy Spirit, let me be full of your Spirit so I can eat the spiritual things from the table God has prepared for me. Let the anointing flow within me to demonstrate your power.

- Fill me with power to lay hands on the sick and let them recover, according to your will.
- Fill me with power to lay hands on those who want to receive the Holy Spirit.
- Fill me with power to speak the oracles of God.
- Fill me with power to decree and declare the promises of God.
- Fill me with your spiritual gifts that destroy the works of the Enemy.
- Fill me with your power to abound in hope, peace, and joy like never before.

Holy Spirit, I receive your godly counsel and the wisdom to make sound decisions and right choices for my life. Give me understanding, and comfort my heart when you instruct me to do certain things. Let the eyes of my understanding be enlightened so I may have full knowledge of God's calling. Do not let anything be hidden from me, and do not let me dwell in ignorance. Reveal to me the secret things concerning the kingdom of God. Shine light in dark areas of my life, and uncover corners that try to confine me in the world's standard and way of living.

Holy Spirit, release in me a new and refreshed spirit every day. Have your way in my life. Thank you for sanctifying me through your spirit. Oh, how I have tasted of the heavenly gift and been made a partaker of you, Holy Spirit. Thank you for being:

- the Spirit of love
- the Spirit of power
- the Spirit of wisdom
- the Spirit of revelation
- the Spirit of faith
- the Spirit of miracles
- the Spirit of heavenly tongues
- the Spirit of discernment
- the Spirit of prophecy

> That their hearts might be comforted, being knit together in love, and unto all riches of the full assurance of understanding, to the acknowledgement of the mystery of God, and of the Father, and of Christ.
> —Colossians 2:2

Spiritual Thoughts

Love creates the passion, and the passion creates the sacrifice. God had a love and passion for us that he sent the ultimate sacrifice (his Son) so he could reach us.

Our passions for prayer also creates a sacrifice. We give up things that are important to us such as sleep, time, schedule, and agenda so we can reach him.

There is a cost associated with a passionate prayer life and a yielding that says, "Not my will, but your will be done."

CHAPTER 3

The Prayer Vessel

> Do you not know that your bodies are temples of the Holy Spirit, who is in you, whom you have received from God? You are not your own.
> —1 Corinthians 6:19 (NIV)

We all have a prayer vessel God has given us called the human body. The body can be considered as our earthly containers, which is also the temple of the Holy Spirit according to the above Scripture. With this in mind, we must understand that our bodies have a heavenly purpose. God created us (mankind) in his likeness and breathed into our nostrils the breath of life. As we know, God is holy and is a spirit, and amazingly, his Holy Spirit dwells within us. We as a people miss this important feature because our spirits are covered up or hidden in our bodies. This is why the Holy Scriptures were written—so we could have knowledge of these things.

> And the LORD God formed man of the dust of the ground, and breathed into his nostrils the breath of life; and man became a living soul.
> —Genesis 2:7

> The spirit of God hath made me, and the breath of the Almighty hath given me life.
> —Job 33:4

Although God created us for his purpose, it is our responsibility to take care of our temples physically and spiritually. One of the most important duties we have is cleansing our temples. This is necessary because the Holy Spirit dwells within our temples. Cleansing impacts the external as well as internal (spiritual). From a spiritual perspective, cleansing is vital to our relationships with God.

There are certain things that can cause us to be unclean. Even though the body itself is physical, every impact to the body can affect us spiritually. When we misuse our physical bodies, we defile our spirits. Therefore, what we do with our bodies can impact our spiritual journeys.

Here's an example. If a person consumes a certain amount of alcohol or other harmful drug, and then attempts to pray, what will be his or her state of mind? This person's internal thought process has been tampered with by the impact of external acts. The tangible things of this nature cannot produce a reaction unless they enter into your body. At that point, they contaminate the spiritual man. The spirit within you was not designed to be altered by anything tangible. The sprit within you was created by the Holy One who breathed into you so you could be holy also. In this case, first we must understand that such things are designed by Satan to defile your body so it cannot be used as a vessel for God.

Satan uses things of this nature to access your spirit and contaminate it with fleshly impurities, causing defilement. He promotes unholy things to disable the authority we have through Christ. God desires us to be pure in our flesh to perfect holiness. Apostle Paul teaches us in 2 Corinthians 7:1 about being cleansed from filthiness of the flesh and spirit: "Having therefore these promises, dearly beloved, let us cleanse ourselves from all filthiness of the flesh and spirit, perfecting holiness in the fear of God."

The body, or vessel, is defiled by what comes out of it, not by what goes into it. When we pray, we do this by speaking outward from our spirits to a holy God. The world will always influence and entice us to keep us from a righteous state with God. This is a tactic to impact our prayers and intercession.

We speak outward from our mouths, which is a part of the vessel, but in most cases, the words come from our hearts. The physical core of the spirit is the heart, and the condition of the heart is made known by the person's words or actions. Matthew talks about us being evil and wonders how we can we speak good things. This tells me that what I allow to enter into my heart, whether it is good or evil, can be spoken out of me. When I engage in intercession, my desire is to speak the will of God, which is good, and the path to speaking good things is to have clean hands and a clean heart. Both of these are significant parts of a vessel that God can use.

> O generation of vipers, how can ye, being evil, speak good things? for out of the abundance of the heart the mouth speaketh.
>
> —Matthew 12:34

Cleansing becomes a requirement for prayer and supplication. Repentance is the starting point for spiritual cleansing. Based on the new covenant, we are cleansed on the inside, even our consciences, through Jesus Christ. He became the sacrifice, and by the shedding of his blood, we can be forgiven of our sins (Hebrew 9:15). We cannot judge how much cleansing is required to clean the heart. Only God, who knows all, can determine what is truly in a person's heart. In addition, Romans 8:27 informs us that the spirit searches the heart before making intercession. We want to approach God always with a clean and sincere heart. God wants us to come to him with sincerity, honesty, and transparency.

> Let us draw near to God with a sincere heart and with the full assurance that faith brings, having our hearts sprinkled to cleanse us from a guilty conscience and having our bodies washed with pure water.
> —Hebrews 10:22

Cleansing allows us to worship and commune with God in spirit and in truth. As we know, not all external impacts are bad for us. An example of an external sign making a good internal impact is water baptism. By confessing our sins and immersing our bodies in the waters of baptism, we believe we have been washed clean on the inside. Cleansing is a crucial part of our prayer lives. When you think about it, why would you want it any other way? The perfect thing about cleansing our hearts is that there is no appointed time. We can ask for forgiveness for anything at any time.

> **Spiritual Thoughts**
>
> Satan is the counterfeiter: everything God designed for good, Satan tries to redesign for bad.
>
> Our bodies were designed to be used by God while here on earth, but Satan wants us to believe that our bodies were made for our own personal use.
>
> We yield to God's design by recognizing that our bodies are the temple of the Holy Spirit and what we do with our bodies is very important to God and our prayer lives.

Defilement

Beware of things that make your body feel good temporarily. Test them by the spirit to define their authorship. Satan will take a two-for-one deal by destroying both the spirit and the body at the same time. Things of this nature go against the purpose and design for which your body was created. Satan knows that the Holy Spirit will not dwell in a place that is unclean (unholy); therefore, intercession is not likely to be fulfilled. So as long as he can get you to defile your temple by what comes out of it, he can eliminate the use of your vessel by God.

> There is nothing from without a man that entering into him can defile him: but the things which come out of him, those are they that defile the man.
> —Mark 7:15

God did not create our bodies to be in a state of defilement but to be vessels he can use to manifest his works here on the earth. There are many forms of defilement. Defile, an action-driven word, can mean corrupt, taint, spoil, tarnish, pollute, ruin, degrade, contaminate, dishonor, desecrate, violate, humiliate, shame, slander, or damage. Merriam-Webster defines the word *defile* as "to make unclean or impure; to corrupt the purity or perfection of, and or to make physically unclean especially with something unpleasant or contaminating."[2] The Word of God takes defilement very seriously because it impacts the heart.

> But those things which proceed out of the mouth come forth from the heart; and they defile the man. For out of the heart proceed evil thoughts, murders, adulteries, fornications, thefts, false witness, blasphemies: These are the things which defile a man: but to eat with unwashen hands defileth not a man.
> —Matthew 15:18–20

In the Old Testament, we find numerous testimonies of defilement and its severe consequences. In Genesis 34, we read that the sons of Jacob, Simeon and Levi, became so angry that they slew Hamor and Shechem and spoiled the city because they had defiled their sister Dinah by raping her. In Numbers 19, we find the story of the unclean man who is cut off from the congregation because his uncleanness defiled the sanctuary of the Lord. Also, in Exodus 31, we are told that the Sabbath is holy, and that everyone who defiles it shall surely be put to death. Thank God for Jesus' grace and mercy!

---

[2] Merriam-Webster's Collegiate Dictionary, Eleventh Edition, 2003

Sin and defilement of the body are closely related. Sin was the reason for the fall of man, and it separated man from God. If sin separated Adam and Eve from God in the beginning of time, it will separate us from God now. However, in Christ, we can repent and be forgiven. This is God's standard, and it will not change. His Word is the same yesterday, today, and forever.

> Know ye not that ye are the temple of God, and that the Spirit of God dwelleth in you? If any man defile the temple of God, him shall God destroy; for the temple of God is holy, which temple ye are.
> —1 Corinthians 3:16–17

> Let not sin therefore reign in your mortal body, that ye should obey it in the lusts thereof.
> —Romans 6:12

Being a vessel God can use to manifest His works here on earth is an important assignment and should not be taken lightly. This type of assignment is birthed through prayer and a personal relationship with God. We know God is all-knowing, all-mighty, and reigns over all creation. Nevertheless, he wants to use us on the earth. Throughout the Scriptures, many people were used for the glory of God, and in most, perhaps all cases, prayer was needed. Several of those Scriptures will be covered in this series.

Our hearts are exceptional organs in our temples. The heart knows everything about us. Every circumstance, situation, thought, and reasoning flows through the heart. Romans 8:27 tells us that God searches our hearts to know the mind of our spirits. This tells me that the heart is what I would call a one-stop shop where our sovereign Lord can go to know the mind of the spirit within that individual.

> And he that searcheth the hearts knoweth what is the mind of the Spirit, because he maketh intercession for the saints according to the will of God.
> —Romans 8:27

The mind of the spirit is captured in our hearts, and that is where God searches for the truth in a matter. This is why it is so crucial that we keep our hearts clean and pure. Spiritual cleansing is a part of holiness that consists of righteousness, repentance, and purging to remove anything that could be a potential hindrance in the relationship an individual has with the Father.

> And thou, Solomon my son, know thou the God of thy father, and serve him with a perfect heart and with a willing mind: for the LORD searcheth all hearts, and understandeth all the imaginations of the thoughts ...
> —1 Chronicles 28:9

> Shall not God search this out? For he knoweth the secrets of the heart.
> —Psalm 44:21

> Create in me a clean heart, O God; and renew a right spirit within me.
> —Psalm 51:10

The Prayer Vessel

I find it quite profound that God knows the secrets of the heart. There is nothing that can be withheld from him. God knows our innermost thoughts and anything we may have hidden in our hearts. The book of Psalms was partly written by King David, a man after God's own heart, who knew and understood the importance of a clean heart. David knew that uncleanness would separate him from God. Because he was a man of repentance and desired a clean heart, God honored his prayers. Throughout Psalms, David wrote many prayers. He did not hesitate to pray and commune with God. Their relationship was birthed through prayer, and David was divinely favored by the Lord.

> As for me, I will call upon God; and the Lord shall save me. Evening, and morning, and at noon, will I pray, and cry aloud: and he shall hear my voice.
> —Psalm 55:16–17

A clean heart will allow God the liberty to work through us, especially in prayer. David also recognized the significance of forgiveness. I believe that more than anything David wanted God to forgive him of his sins because this was an essential part of cleansing his heart. God sent his only begotten Son so we could be forgiven of our sins, which is why it is so important that we, too, forgive. Forgiveness is a vital key with God; our relationships with him are based on it.

> I the Lord search the heart, I try the reins, even to give every man according to his ways, and according to the fruit of his doings.
> —Jeremiah 17:10

KINGDOM INTERCESSION

I believe prayer is one of the divine designs God created within us because it allows the Holy Spirit to make intercession with the Father in heaven for us while we are here on earth. Our bodies should always reflect the spirit within us. What happens within our spiritual lives should be mirrored outwardly. We are speaking spirits that God has deposited in earthly bodies. The same creator of heaven and earth has designed each of us uniquely for prayer and intercession. Kingdom intercession and prayers are built on our personal relationships with God. They reflect his will for our lives. The Holy Spirit is always in perfect agreement with the will of God.

CHAPTER 4

Spiritual Vision

Then He turned to His disciples and said privately,
Blessed are the eyes which see the things you see.
—Luke 10:23

It is a blessing to have eyes to see but more so to have eyes that allow you to see the kingdom of God being manifested on earth. In the above Scripture reading, Jesus is telling the disciples they have been chosen to see his great works. The prophets and kings of the past truly desired to see the things that were prophesized but did not live to see them. I can only imagine how it feels to have a prophecy birthed out of you yet not live to see it transpire.

The disciples were blessed to witness the miracles, signs, and wonders performed by Jesus himself. We are blessed to share what they saw by reading the Scriptures. As we read and apply the Word, it allows us to see how God works spiritually, as manifested in the natural. We become witnesses to the truth also.

Seeing from a kingdom perspective is having our eyes of understanding enlightened so we see with spiritual eyes. The things of God are beyond our natural understanding. Therefore, we must first be open to receive the truth when we hear it. Jesus taught the truth! He was here on earth only for a short period of time, and there was no reason or purpose to portray anything that was not of God the Father.

> God is not a man, that he should lie; neither the son of man, that he should repent: hath he said, and shall he not do it? Or hath he spoken, and shall he not make it good?
>
> —Numbers 23:19

Our prayer request should be that God gives us spiritual eyes to see and understand spiritual things. We should desire to see his glory in all things. His messages are too great to be missed for lack of vision. They are written to reveal the truth. His wisdom and knowledge are revealed only to those who have a desire to see. When we pray, our vision becomes one with the Holy Spirit, and we can see God moving and working things out.

Our eyes shall be a witness to God when the Scriptures come to life. Just like the disciples, we are witnesses to the Messiah. We can witness that the Word of God is factual and authentic because the truth has been revealed and is still being demonstrated in our lives today. When our eyes witness the same miracles, signs, and wonders, we receive confirmation of what God is doing even in this very hour. The power of God works through us to heal the sick, cause the blind to see (naturally and spiritually), or cast out demons to set captives free. The power of God working through us can be increased through kingdom intercession with the Father; even Jesus interceded with the Father. Being the Son of God, I can only imagine that Jesus' intercession was from a kingdom perspective, and more so now, for he is seated at the right hand of the Father in his kingdom.

> And Jesus said, I am: and ye shall see the Son of man sitting on the right hand of power, and coming in the clouds of heaven.
> —Mark 14:62

> It is Christ that died, yea rather, that is risen again, who is even at the right hand of God, who also maketh intercession for us.
> —Romans 8:34

When a person can "see" spiritually and really understand the power of God, things appear in an elevated perspective. God is not giving us a new thing but manifesting what He already gave us in the beginning. God gave us dominion over this earth, and we have the authority and the freedom to walk in this blessing. However, if we do not have eyes to see and believe in our hearts, we cannot operate in this power. There is no reason for any of God's children to be bound by sin when they can have knowledge of the truth that concerns the purpose of their lives.

Our eyes are the gateway to our hearts. The Bible tells us in Proverbs 4:23 to guard our hearts for everything we do flows from them. We should also be cautious of what we expose our eyes to since they are an entry point. Temptation is a tactic Satan uses to provoke us to sin. When we have our eyes open for spiritual insight, we should be able to see temptation coming long before it arrives. Spiritual eyes detect sin before we ever indulge in it. Our spiritual eyes protect the heart. If sin can get past the eyes and into the heart, its seed is planted within us. Therefore, we should be on the alert in our surroundings at all times. For me, spiritual vision was birthed through consistent intercession with my Abba Father.

When I decided that I was going to live my life for Christ, the Enemy used many diverse tactics to try to derail me off my course. As a fallen angel, Satan recognizes and understands the spiritual things of God; therefore, he knows if we have obtained our spiritual vision. I believe that is one of the first things he looks for when forming attacks against us. He likes it when we are blinded to his works.

The Enemy knew it was my desire to live a righteous life for Christ. Being a single woman, he also knew I desired to be married, so he formed distractions to throw me off course. He knew my past, and using our pasts against us is one of his most popular weapons. During this time, the adversary was fully aware that I could only see in the natural. He knew this because he studies us to see what we like and don't like, and most of all, he listens closely to the things we say before he entices us.

A consistent prayer life will change the things you say, the things you like, and the way you see. Many times, we miss the signs God shows us because we are quick to deviate to what we *want* to see. I strongly believe that Satan studied Eve before approaching her.

As I mentioned earlier, during this time, I had a desire to be married. The Enemy used this to create a maze in my life. I was opening the wrong doors and trying to make something happen without the counsel of God. My first mistake was trying to build a relationship with someone else when I had not yet built my relationship with God. I had not established a prayer life, and as a result, I could not see what the Enemy was doing.

Behind each door was a different type of man, yet in many ways, they were all the same. My spiritual vision was impaired and so were my spiritual steps. Because I could not see, I started walking into doors of compromise, not realizing that I was waging warfare in my life. My lack of knowledge and the temptations of this world were leading me into a deadly web of destruction. Spiritual blindness can cost us something more valuable than anything this world could ever offer. The world can never give us eternal life; it can only lie to us by offering it. When we cannot see spiritually, we are at the mercy of the Enemy. In my situation, the Enemy was using me because I could not see spiritually. Making wrong choices in life not only hurt me but others as well.

My reason for sharing my experience is to help someone else. Being transparent comes not only with spiritual vision but with spiritual maturity as well. Although I wanted to live a righteous life, I was still blind. We all need spiritual eyes that not only see the works of God but also the works of the Enemy.

Satan is a counterfeiter and knows how to disguise things so you cannot see what is lying beneath. This is what happened to Eve in the garden of Eden. Satan used the body of the serpent so Eve could not see him. He changed her view. Deception is his game, and sometimes he deals a winning hand if we do not seek God for our spiritual vision. Sometimes these painful experiences of spiritual blindness come when we are trying to get closer to God. I believe God tests our vision at times to see if we are viewing the signs and warnings he sends before proceeding. The signs are always there; we just need insight to see them.

Our noses and eyes need to work in unison so we do not fall into the hands of the Enemy without knowing it. The nose is the discerner; it can smell something miles away even before it comes into view.

One thing I have learned about Satan: he always manifests himself in some form or fashion. He always says or does something that is contrary to God. That should be your cue to take a closer look, using your spiritual insight. Spiritual vision is important to God.

Apostle Paul (Saul) lost his physical vision so it could be restored to glorify the Father. God used the one tool that was assisting Saul in his evil works. Saul's vision of Christians was distorted, leading him to hate them. God took away his sight, so Saul could no longer pursue evil. Before losing his sight, the last thing Saul saw was a light from heaven. He heard the voice of Jesus telling him that he was going to witness for him. Jesus also told him that he was going to send him to open the eyes of the people, to turn them from darkness and the power of Satan. God was not only going to restore Paul's physical vision but also open his spiritual vision.

> I will rescue you from your own people and from the Gentiles. I am sending you to them to open their eyes and turn them from darkness to light and from the power of Satan to God, so that they may receive forgiveness of sins and a place among those who are sanctified by faith in me.
>
> —Acts 26:17–18 (NIV)

It is written that Jesus is the truth (John 14:6). His words were pure, honest, and just, and the Father spoke to him through intercessory prayer. The intimate time Jesus spent with the Father was precious because it was on a kingdom level. Those prayers had to be meaningful and straight to the point. I do not believe Jesus would have wasted valuable moments on things that were not relevant to his purpose. So their communication had to be of one accord because of God's plan. The Father and the Son knew and understood each other

Spiritual Vision

perfectly, and there was no ambiguity concerning their identity or purpose.

> All things are delivered to me of my Father: and no man knoweth who the Son is, but the Father; and who the Father is, but the Son, and he to whom the Son will reveal him.
>
> —Luke 10:22

Our eyes have to witness who Christ is. As we grow and learn the Scriptures, we see Jesus revealed as the Messiah. Merriam-Webster describes the term *Messiah* as the expected king and deliverer of the Jews.[3] Jesus is the expected King and Messiah. He bore the sins of mankind and was resurrected so we could live. We are witnesses for Christ because we continue to see his works in action.

As we see God operating through his Word and allow it to saturate our spirits, we can witness the Word to others. When the Word of God is planted in our spirits, we begin to understand his language, which is compatible with our spirits. So when we hear it, we begin to understand God's ways. Our human ways are meaningless and of no significance to kingdom living. Isaiah 55:8 tells us that God's thoughts are not our thoughts; neither are our ways his ways. The more we see God working and operating in our lives, the more we see how things can work together for the good.

Another example of spiritual eyes opening through intercession is the story of the prophet Elisha. He had a double portion of spiritual vision because God had imparted a double portion of Elijah's anointing on Elisha. Therefore, Elisha's eyes were opened spiritually, and when this occurred, he wanted others to see spiritually also. One thing

---

[3] Merriam-Webster's Collegiate Dictionary, Eleventh Edition, 2003

we must understand is that spiritual vision does not come without a relationship with God for his glory. As mentioned before, there are many gifts, but one spirit. In this passage, the anointing of Elisha's prayer was so powerful that it had impact in three separate instances:

> And when the servant of the man of God was risen early, and gone forth, behold, an host compassed the city both with horses and chariots. And his servant said unto him, Alas, my master! how shall we do?
>
> And he answered, Fear not: for they that be with us are more than they that be with them.
>
> And Elisha prayed, and said, LORD, I pray thee, open his eyes, that he may see. And the LORD opened the eyes of the young man; and he saw: and, behold, the mountain was full of horses and chariots of fire round about Elisha.
>
> And when they came down to him, Elisha prayed unto the LORD, and said, Smite this people, I pray thee, with blindness. And he smote them with blindness according to the word of Elisha.
>
> And Elisha said unto them, This is not the way, neither is this the city: follow me, and I will bring you to the man whom ye seek. But he led them to Samaria.
>
> And it came to pass, when they were come into Samaria, that Elisha said, LORD, open the eyes of these men, that they may see. And the LORD opened their

eyes, and they saw; and, behold, they were in the midst of Samaria.

—2 Kings 6:15-20

- First, Elisha prayed to the Lord to open his servant's eyes so he might see that the mount was full of horses and chariots. God opened his eyes, and his servant saw this "vision in the spirit."
- Second, Elisha then prayed for God to smite the people with blindness so they could not see where they were going. Again, when you cannot see spiritually, your spiritual walk or direction is impaired. God honored Elisha's prayer and smote them with blindness and led them in another direction.
- Third, Elisha prayed again for God to open the eyes of the men that they might see. The Lord opened their eyes, and they saw that they were in the midst of Samaria.

Kingdom intercession can bring forth spiritual vision. Elisha was seeking the kingdom of heaven to be made manifest on earth through prayer. Interceding on behalf of others is the will of God for his people in order to fulfill his purpose and plans on the earth. Opening the servant's eyes allowed faith and trust in God to prevail over the circumstances and situation.

Kingdom Intercession: Prayer for Spiritual Vision

Our Father who is in heaven, you are great in all your ways. The magnitude of your wisdom is without measure. Your name is Jehovah. You created our eyes and are the giver of spiritual vision. Holy, divine, and wonderful God, we worship you in spirit and in truth.

Father, we thank you for sending your Son to bear our sins so we could have everlasting life, which is the ultimate vision of your will. Forgive us for our trespasses and anything we did that was not pleasing to you. Forgive us for being blinded by the things of this world.

Holy Father, we come before you asking you to open our eyes to see your light and glory. We ask that you remove our spiritual blindness as you did for Paul so we might see spiritual things as never before. We want to see your divine purpose and will for our lives.

Father, give us a greater understanding; allow us to be true witnesses in our hearts. Uncover things that have been hidden from us by the residue of this world. Show us your glory as we seek you for our spiritual vision:

- to see beyond our natural vision;
- to see you in every situation and circumstance;
- to see you intertwining, weaving, unlocking, and connecting us to your power;
- to see your Spirit reigning like never before, overpowering anything that is not like you;
- to see your Holy Spirit dwelling in us, guiding, teaching, and instructing;
- to see spiritual visions and prophecies manifested in the earth;
- to see the Spirit of God moving among us;
- to see the Enemy's plot, plan, tactic, and every weapon being formed against us in the spirit;
- to see in the spirit realm as a lamp that brings light to dark places.

Father, as you release our spiritual vision, let the eyes of our understanding be enlightened also:

- to fully understand the truth concerning the Father, Son, and Holy Spirit;
- to fully understand the Great Commission;
- to fully understand everlasting and eternal life through Christ;
- to fully understand the power of the Holy Spirit;
- to fully understand the greatest commandment of love;
- to fully understand your authority on the earth;
- to fully understand the end times;
- to fully understand the kingdom of God.

In Jesus' name we pray. Amen.

CHAPTER 5

Praying the Divine Target

*P*raying targeted prayers is a kingdom practice. In the pursuit of a kingdom mind-set, we should strive to be successful in our prayer lives. Our desires should be to pray bountiful prayers that are full of life and purpose. The Word of God is life, and when we pray the Word, we are speaking words of power. There are many prayers written in the Holy Scriptures, and we can include them in our prayers, for we read in 2 Timothy 3:16, "All scripture is given by inspiration of God, and is profitable for doctrine, for reproof, for correction, for instruction in righteousness."

When engaging in kingdom prayer and intercession, there is a focal point we should adhere to. I refer to this as a Prayer Mission Statement, which is: "Thy will be done." Our prayer centers should always be about God's will being done on earth as it is in heaven. I believe that when we pray God's will, we have his ear.

> And he said unto them, When ye pray, say, Our Father which art in heaven, Hallowed be thy name. Thy

> kingdom come. Thy will be done, as in heaven, so in earth.
>
> —Luke 11:2

Praying targeted prayers brings forth results. When you aim your prayers directly at something, you are more likely to hit the target rather than praying amiss.

There are major keys to successful prayer and intercession. Two of those keys are prayer purpose and prayer objectives. There can be several objectives, but only one purpose. The overarching purpose for kingdom prayer and intercession should be to seek the will of God above all else. When we commune with God, we constantly renew our minds toward spiritual things, which allows us to pray effectively.

God's will is the road map to the prayer purpose, and the objectives should represent Christ. Jesus told us in the Scriptures that he is the way, the truth, and the life. No one comes unto the Father except through him. This includes our prayer protocol.

> And the Word was made flesh, and dwelt among us, (and we beheld his glory, the glory as of the only begotten of the Father,) full of grace and truth.
>
> —John 1:14

> Jesus saith unto him, I am the way, the truth, and the life: no man cometh unto the Father, but by me.
>
> —John 14:6

Jesus was and still is the example we are to follow. He was with God not only in the beginning but while he was on this earth, showing us the way to the Father. He prayed diligently and earnestly to the

Father, seeking his will even until death. Jesus gave instructions on how to pray, and they were always toward the divine target. "Thy kingdom come" means God's will. "Kingdom" represents God, not so much as a geological place, but a spiritual place. The intent of prayer is not to change what God has already created in heaven but for earth to be *as* heaven. In other words, we do not change heaven, but heaven changes us. So our prayers ought to represent what heaven is. In heaven, there is no sickness, distress, lack, or death. Most of all, Satan simply cannot and will not ever operate there.

Praying the divine target means working with the Holy Spirit to use tactical praying methods to hit pivotal points in your prayer dialogue. Further in this chapter, you will see several targeted prayers that can be included in kingdom intercession. These are in alignment with the spiritual objectives mentioned earlier. Praying targeted prayers can assist with building up your prayer life as it draws you closer to the Father. Seeking the will of God will bring you to a position where God can use you more than ever.

The Word of God contains everything we need to pray his divine will. Remember, the mission is not our will, but his.

Kingdom Intercession: To Proclaim

Prayer target: Proclaiming who God is.
Meditation Scriptures: Genesis 1; Exodus 33:17–23; Jeremiah 17:5–12; Luke 9:1–6

Our Father in heaven, we proclaim that you are the great I Am, gracious and merciful God. There is none like you. You are great in all your ways, mighty and powerful. Your immeasurable wisdom and strength is beyond the thoughts of man.

Let your goodness pass before us. We proclaim your greatness. We pray that your will be done in the lives of your people. We stand at the gate of your presence proclaiming that you are holy, sovereign, majestic, wise, and righteous. The brilliance of your glory is so vast and vibrant that darkness cannot comprehend it.

Father,
- we proclaim that your Word is true and does not return void. It is quick, powerful, and sharper than any two-edged sword; the sword of the Spirit. Let your Word go forth and create, heal, deliver, set free, and save your people;
- we proclaim that your anointing surpasses the works of the Enemy and breaks the yokes of bondage. Father, anoint and consecrate your sons and daughters so we might tell of your kingdom and feed your flock;
- we proclaim that you are our spiritual covering. Cover your people in your garment of praise, for it is light, unlike the spirit of heaviness;
- we proclaim freedom and peace in our land. You are the God of peace and righteousness who heals our land as we humble ourselves in prayer while seeking your face as we turn from our wicked ways. We thank you for allowing us to possess the land you have promised us;
- we proclaim you are righteous and desire us to be trees of righteousness for your glory;
- we proclaim liberty to the captives who are bound by the works of Satan. We command that God's people be loosed from the chains, shackles, and handcuffs of the Enemy;
- we proclaim the restored authority on earth over those bound by evil spirits and demons. Loose them now in the name of

Jesus! Father, you are peace. Fill them with your peace so their spirits can be at rest; and
- we proclaim the good news of the kingdom of God. The gospel of the kingdom and the healing of every infirmity. Your kingdom is not of this world, but we pray for its coming. We glorify you.

In Jesus' name we pray. Amen.

Kingdom Intercession: To Repent

Prayer target: To turn away from evil and all abominations and obey God's commands.
Meditation Scriptures: Ezekiel 14:6; Exodus 20:1–17; Psalm 51; Galatians 5

Our Father in heaven, we come to you with our prayers of repentance. We pray that you will have mercy on us, dear Lord, for our trespasses. We pray that you will forgive us and blot out our transgressions against you.

We trust and believe in your Word and acknowledge that it is true and full of life. Purge us with hyssop so our vessels can be cleansed. Hide our faces from the sins of this world, and mark out our iniquities.

Give us a clean heart, O Lord, and renew a true spirit within us. We acknowledge that Jesus died for our sins so we can be forgiven. Yet we still sin against you.

Father,
- we repent of worshipping other gods before you and for putting the temporal things of this world ahead of you. We

made idols and chose riches above everlasting life because of our lack of understanding. Please do not turn your ear away from us, but pardon our sins, O Sovereign God;

- we repent of denying the deity of your Son, Jesus. For not believing what the Holy Scriptures proclaim and allowing the world to dictate and penetrate our thinking. Help us to turn away from our carnal thinking and unbelief. Thank you for sending your Son to die for our sins;
- we repent of not loving and trusting you completely. Fill our hearts with an unconditional love that embraces the multitude. Great is your faithfulness;
- we repent of not adhering to your holy statutes and commands. Train us concerning your ordinances and the lifestyle we should live. We want to please you;
- we repent of not honoring our mothers and fathers as your Scriptures instruct so our days are long upon the land that you have given us. We recognize your instructions and aim to correct where we have fallen short;
- we repent of assailing character, reputation, and integrity of our brothers and sisters by speaking negatively of them based on our own likes and dislikes. You are God, our judge, and vengeance is yours. Let us know a man by his spirit;
- we repent of committing adultery, spiritually and physically. Jesus spoke of spiritual adultery and said that great tribulation would come unless we repent. Forgive us for physically defiling your design for marriage—holy matrimony;
- we repent of stealing what does not belong rightfully to us. We have even robbed you, God, and pray for your leniency and compassion. Instill in us a new heart of giving;

- we repent for bearing false witness against our brothers and sisters. We have allowed our tongues to speak lies rather than righteousness. Deliver our souls, O Lord, from lying lips and a deceitful tongue;
- we repent of coveting anything that does not belong to us. Grant us wisdom to seek first the kingdom of God and your righteousness, for all things shall be added unto us; and
- we repent because the kingdom of heaven is at hand! Father, please forgive us so we can inherit your kingdom of God.

In Jesus' name we pray. Amen.

Kingdom Intercession: To Cry Out

Prayer target: Interceding and crying out for God to hear our prayers
Meditation Scriptures: Daniel 9:4–19; Genesis 4; 2 Chronicles 20:9; Matthew 2; Psalms 17:1; Lamentations 2:19

Our Father in heaven, we cry out to you to hear the prayers and petitions of your servants. We are not perfect in our ways and do not have the full knowledge of you. We have not obeyed your voice. Father, we cry out to you with a sincere heart as we seek your face to shine upon your people. Have mercy on those who love you and keep your commandments.

Incline your ear and hear our cries. We are your people to whom you have given life. In deep admiration and reverence for you, we do not present our supplications before you based on our righteousness but on your great mercies.

Father,

KINGDOM INTERCESSION

- we cry out to you, O Lord, to give ear to our prayers that do not come from fake lips but earnestly seek you with authenticity;
- we cry out with a righteous cry to have mercy on us and deliver us from evil. Our trust is in you, all-powerful God. Detach and free us from things that do not give you glory;
- we cry out to you with a loud and a bitter cry from the wiles of this life. We are your people and the sheep in your pasture. Save us from the violence of this world. Let every weapon formed against your people fall to the ground and never prosper in the name of Jesus;
- we cry out to you as Hannah did for the children. Shield them from evil and from the dark things of this world. Seal and protect their minds from toxic seeds sown by the prince of this world. Tear down every plot and plan designed to destroy our future;
- we cry out to you for impartations of godly wisdom and knowledge among the children so they will understand spiritual things and their purpose in life. We rebuke every King Manasseh and Herod spirit that sheds innocent blood. We lift up the children to you for shelter and safety from the hands of Satan;
- we cry out to you for the safety of our families and loved ones you have ordained for us. You have handpicked each of our family members. We rebuke the spirit of division that causes separation. You are the glue that holds us together. Teach us to love one another more and demolish every Cain spirit that comes to kill and destroy the family;
- we cry out to you for the security of our personages and properties with which you have blessed us. Place a hedge

around the borders and parameters of the land you have given us. Do not let the Enemy poison our fruits or spoil our goods;
- we cry out in the midnight hour for your people; the three a.m. hour, the six and nine a.m. hours, to disarm the schemes and designs of the Evil One. Let every demonic plan crumble to the ground;
- we cry out to you when darkness comes upon us as a sword, judgment, pestilence, or famine. We stand steadfast in your presence with sincere prayers of faith, knowing that you hear the cry of your people and will not hide your face from us but help us in these afflictions; and
- we cry out and shout with joy, for great is the holy God who is in the midst of our prayers and intercession.

In Jesus' name we pray. Amen.

Kingdom Intercession: To Reveal

Prayer target: The glory of God be revealed
Meditation Scriptures: Isaiah 40:5–8; Psalm 8, 19, 104; Ephesians 1:17–18

Our Father in heaven, reveal your glory to all flesh. O Lord, how excellent is your name in all the earth. You have set your glory above the heavens. The revealed glory of God exceeds any conceivable wisdom. It is your glory that brings light to the simplest things in the universe.

We pray that our eyes of understanding will be unwrapped, that we might see the glory of God operating in our lives. Your glory is indescribable. The core of your wisdom that represents your glory shines brighter than any consumable light.

Father, your Son beholds your glory. The revealed light of Christ Jesus is more valuable than rubies and other precious jewels.

Father,
- reveal more of the secret things concerning your kingdom. Give us understanding as you teach us how to dive through multilayered revelation and knowledge;
- reveal more of the hidden wisdom of your Holy Scriptures. Bring every parable to the light of comprehension to help us grow;
- reveal to your people how to be faithful servants of the Lord. Shine light in areas of confusion and misunderstanding;
- reveal the darkness in every area of our lives so we can walk in the light of Christ;
- reveal and expose every power, principality, ruler of the darkness, and spiritual wickedness in high places. Disclose their traps, plots, and plans that cause your people to stumble and fall. Divulge their deceptive tactics, and shatter their stumbling blocks out of our paths. Give us spiritual vision to see in the spirit when weapons are being formed against us so they can be disarmed;
- reveal and uncover financial webs that entangle and bind your people in debt. Release economic insight with strategic impartations of kingdom investments;
- reveal spiritual assignments with road maps to accomplish your will;
- reveal deeper revelation of dreams and visions given to us in the midnight hour. Let us awake with full understanding and interpretations;

- reveal the wicked ones and the danger of ungodly relationships. Bring to light the examples in your Scriptures so we can see and understand that there is nothing new under the sun; and
- reveal to your intercessors spiritual things beyond the spheres of this world. Make known to them the profound greatness of your creativity.

In Jesus' name we pray. Amen.

Kingdom Intercession: To Remove and Heal

Prayer target: For healing
Meditation Scriptures: Isaiah 53:5; Malachi 4:2; Matthew 12:15, 14:14, 15:30

Our Father in heaven, we confess that Jesus was wounded for our transgressions, bruised for our iniquities, and the chastisement of our peace was upon him. By his stripes we are healed.

It is written that the Son of righteousness would arise with healing in his wings. We pray that the gospel of the kingdom and healing of all sickness and disease among your people will continue to be manifested on the earth. Let the prayers of your people remain effectual and fervent so we may always have your ear.

We thank you that, above all things, you desire us to prosper and be in good health, even as our souls prosper. Anoint us to stretch forth our hands and heal your people in the name of Jesus so you can be glorified.

Father,
- heal your people of all diseases and bring their bodies back into the order of your created design:

- Remove all types and forms of cancer.
- Remove all types and forms of blood diseases.
- Remove all types and forms of lung diseases.
- Remove all types and forms of heart and brain diseases.
- Remove all types and forms of intestinal diseases.
- Remove all types and forms of infectious diseases.
- Remove all types and forms of bacterial diseases.
- Remove all types and forms of cell diseases.
- Remove all types and forms of skin diseases.
- Remove all types and forms of organ diseases.
- Remove all types and forms of rare diseases.
- Remove all types and forms of airborne diseases.
- Remove all types and forms of contagious diseases.
- Remove all types and forms of environmental diseases.
- Remove all types and forms of curable and non-curable diseases.

- heal, O Lord, for many are weak in their bodies, worried in their minds, and tired of the Enemy attacking their souls. Renew their strength and restore the time spent in suffering and distress;
- heal our land so it can bring forth fruit. We want to be humble, prayerful, and righteous. Let us turn from all forms of wickedness to seek your face;
- heal our souls from darkness; remove any soul ties that have caused us to go astray. We have sinned against you, but we pray your love will cover us;
- heal us, God, as you deliver us from destruction. Redirect our paths to your purpose. Wipe our wounds, mend our sores, and remove our pain;

- heal the brokenhearted, dry our tears, repair what has been torn, and give us peace in our spirits;
- heal those who have an issue of blood. Reveal and impart into them that their bodies are the temple of the Holy Spirit. We declare that our bodies are a living sacrifice unto you;
- heal our ears that we may hear. Remove the damaged, ill-spoken, and ungodly words we have heard; and
- heal our nations one by one, name by name. We decree and declare that we are a holy nation.

Father, we bind Satan right now in the name of Jesus! Remove every infirmity, assassinate every seed of infirmity, exterminate every branch of infirmity, and dissolve every residue of infirmity. Destroy every curse, wicked design, and plan of infirmity right now in the name of Jesus Christ of Nazareth. Loose the miracles and your healing power right now in the bodies of your people who have been impacted by the trespasses and works of Satan.

In Jesus' name we pray. Amen.

Kingdom Intercession: To Destroy

Prayer target: Spiritual intercession to destroy the works of the Enemy
Meditation Scriptures: Job 34:21–27; Ezekiel 28:12–19; Luke 10:19; James 2:19; 1 John 3:8

Our Father in heaven, you have given us assignments to pray over the nations and over the kingdoms, to destroy and to build, to pull down and to erect, to root out and to plant.

The Enemy's goal is to kill, steal, and destroy your people and to make our land desolate. The instruments of evil are designed to tear down and slaughter the righteous with weapons of destruction. Evil seeks to devour your holy temples by means of enticing temptations of worldly riches, but we decree that evil shall not break up your holy mountain.

Purify your altars and sanctify what belongs to you. You are the great Jehovah and shall not be moved!

Father,
- destroy the works of Satan so they shall know that you are the Lord God;
- destroy the kingdom of darkness that opposes your kingship. Let the kingdom of God reign;
- destroy perversion. Eliminate every twisted, corrupt, and filthy-minded spirit causing your people to operate in sin. Impart your righteousness and holiness in the lives of your people to restore chastity and purity;
- destroy divination. Demolish soothsaying, witchcraft, and every enchanting spirit in the name of Jesus. Replace these evil spirits with your spirit of faith and trust;
- destroy fear. Exterminate seeds of torment, phobias, nightmares, mental anxiety, and, most of all, fear of death. In you there is everlasting life. Impart peace, love, and a sound mind within your people;
- destroy infirmity and all other diseases planted by Satan. Make internal disorders and sicknesses vanish, never to return. Evaporate oppression, depression, and any forms of evil that cause misery and despair among your people. Let their bodies be restored to the original design you created;
- destroy every tree of evil and the fruit thereof. Cut them off from the land of the living. Consume every wicked root, sinful branch, and deceptive leaf. Father, replace and plant

trees of righteousness with roots of life, branches of truth, and leaves that multiply and replenish the earth;
- destroy every murderous weapon formed against us. Trash the fiery missiles sent to terminate the promises and blessing you have planned for us. Gird us with your armor and shield of protection;
- destroy the prince assigned to tear down our nation. Extinguish his plans, plots, and schemes from the face of the earth. Overthrow the spiritual wickedness in high places that seduces our spirits with flattering lies. Let the counsel of evil principalities be terminated immediately. Let us be a holy nation; and
- destroy the works of the prince whose aim is to dominate the atmosphere. Suppress the seeds of evil that are sown in the spirit. Utterly destroy those armies who never sleep, whose mission, like that of a predator, seeks to devour us. Father, lift the sword against every airborne evil spirit. We decree and declare that your Holy Spirit is releasing in the atmosphere your power, wisdom, healing, and truth to continue destroying the works of the Enemy.

In Jesus' name we pray. Amen.

Kingdom Intercession: Hide Us

Prayer target: Asking God to hide and protect us in the shadow of His wings
Meditation Scriptures: Deuteronomy 11:6; Isaiah 59:19; Psalm 1:1–3, 17:8, 32:7, 119:114

Our Father in heaven, you are our hiding place. You protect us from trouble and surround us with songs of deliverance. Continue to instruct and teach us in the way we should go. Your wings shield us from the Evil One. Your Word tells us that the Enemy will come in like a flood, but the Spirit of the Lord shall lift up a standard against him to defend us.

Watch over and provide us with your holy counsel. You are God, the creator whose Spirit moves upon the face of the earth, watching day and night. Nothing goes on without your knowledge because you are an all-seeing God.

In your hiding place, our souls rest on green pastures of peace. In this place, there are still waters that restore our souls as the path of righteousness stretches out before us. The gates of hell cannot prevail against your hiding place.

Father,
- hide us from the wiles of this world and keep us fastened tightly to your will;
- hide us from the multitude of temptations and the enticement of sin;
- hide us from scorn and the sneer of those who hate you;
- hide us from the ungodly counsel of the wicked and the rebellious workers of iniquity;
- hide us when you pour your wrath upon the wicked;
- hide us when the death angel passes by our dwellings;
- hide us when you execute judgment, when the winds blow fiercely, when the seas rage angrily, when the mouth of the earth is opened forcefully, and when your consuming fire comes to destroy;

- hide the Word of God deep in our hearts so the adversary cannot snatch it away from us;
- hide our properties and possessions from the thief who comes to steal, kill, and destroy;
- hide us from ignorance while you shape us in wisdom; and
- hide us in times of trouble when our knees buckle until we are able to stand strong again.

In Jesus' name we pray. Amen.

Kingdom Intercession: To Restore

Prayer target: Restoration of the mind, body, and soul
Meditation Scriptures: Job 42:10; Proverbs 30:11–14; Isaiah 61:3; Jeremiah 29:11; Joel 2:25–26

Our Father in heaven, we yearn for your presence. We seek your face and all that is pure. You are the Most High, and we worship you.

You are the great restorer of all times. Repair our souls from the weather and storms of this world. Reinstate our rightful position with you. Repair our minds from the deformed way of thinking that has been generationally imparted.

Reverse the curse on your people from our rebellious and stubborn forefathers. Recondition our bodies to be a living sacrifice, holy and sacred unto you. Renovate the inner chambers of our hearts so we can worship you in spirit and in truth. Rebuild our spirits as sons and daughters of righteousness.

Father,
- restore your plans for the people to inherit the kingdom of God;

- restore our land to peace and let if bring forth much fruit so we may eat from your table continually;
- restore all that is lost in storms and in empty seasons of hardship;
- restore what has been violently taken away from us, those things deceitfully plundered by the coveter;
- restore to your people the years lost to the locust, cankerworm, caterpillar, and palmerworm. Fill our days with blessings. No longer will the Enemy smite our prosperity;
- restore all that is rightfully ours, the fruit of the trees, the wheat of the fields, and all that was spoiled when we left the land of milk and honey;
- restore peace and rest in our spirits while we await your return;
- restore confidence when we cannot see you moving in our favor. Rebuild our trust in you and your mighty works;
- restore the anointing oil on our heads to renew our souls. Anoint our hands, mouths, and feet to fulfill your will;
- restore our garments of praise, now covered with hurt and pain. Refurbish the garment to create an atmosphere of praise and exaltation;
- restore our oil of joy and gladness so our torn spirits can be mended again;
- restore your people, reestablish them in your sight, and replace the faith that was lost; and
- restore our spiritual sight. Father, let our eyes of understanding be enlightened so we can discern spiritual things about the kingdom of God.

In Jesus' name we pray. Amen.

Kingdom Intercession: To Transform

Prayer target: Be transformed in the ways and statutes of God
Meditation Scriptures: Matthew 6:33; Romans 12:2; Ephesians 4:11, 5:2, 5:8; Colossians 1:18; Revelation 1:4–20

Our Father in heaven, we pray that you transform the mind-set and ways of your people. Transform the multitude! The blind cannot see because they do not know they are blind. Dissolve the specks in their eyes so they might see what you see. Transfigure them to be what you created them to be.

You are the Spirit of truth, and we pray that you transform those fallen apostles who support vain and deceitful works in your church, those who do not adhere to the letters John wrote to the seven churches in the book of Revelation. Transform them to be true apostles of Christ.

Father,
- transform prophets who prophesy false visions, divinations, idolatries, and delusions of their own minds with unclean lips. They are ignorant to accountability and the blood on their hands. Transform them, touch their lips to remove their iniquity, and purge their sins. Command them to speak the truth forevermore so you can use them for the kingdom of God;
- transform evangelists who refuse to follow your commands, ways, and, most of all, the assignments you have given them. Give them wisdom and knowledge of the true meaning of provision. Give them an obedient spirit, and baptize them again with the gift of faith as you resend them forth;

- transform pastors who are deceiving your flock by turning your churches into a den of thieves, using your holy offerings for self gain, and not taking care of the poor, widowed, and fatherless. They have been stained by the world. Retrain them to be good shepherds of your flock by feeding those who hunger and thirst for you;
- transform teachers of the law into teachers of your kingdom. Transform their worldly teaching methods and their flattering words of influence with spiritual wisdom that shatters the spirit of error;
- transform and revamp your churches to your original plan and purpose. Let us not fall into the destruction of darkness and make a mockery of God, but fear him;
- transform us to be a chosen generation, royal priesthood, holy nation, and a peculiar people so we should show forth the praises of him who has called us out of darkness into his marvelous light;
- transform us to be good stewards. Give us wisdom in our finances;
- transform us to have a kingdom mind-set with understanding of spiritual things;
- transform us to seek the will of God so we may silence the ignorant and foolish things of this world;
- transform us to respect the liberty you have given us. Being free, but not using your authority to go before you and pave our own way. Teach us to be upstanding servants of God;
- transform us to be stronger intercessors, prayer warriors, gatekeepers, and watchmen on the wall. Let us be transfigured from glory to glory so that when we pray your image inside of us may manifest your purposes and plans;

- transform our thinking so we may have clear understanding that Jesus is the head of the body, which is the church, and has preeminence in all things;
- transform our thoughts to be as pure and transparent as glass. Help us keep our thinking and intellect on the things of Christ to prevent the Enemy from having access to our minds, causing us to entertain evil;
- transform our prayers into kingdom intercession so we may surrender our will to your will and allow you to speak through us to manifest your works here on earth;
- transform our hearing and make adjustments to our ears so we may hear your voice with comprehensive understanding. We want to hear you with precision and simplicity; and
- transform us by renewing our minds so we may know what is good, acceptable, and perfect according to the will of God.

In Jesus' name we pray. Amen.

Kingdom Intercession: Let There Be

Prayer target: Speaking life with the power of God in prayer
Meditation Scripture: Genesis 1

Our Father in heaven, in the beginning you created heaven and earth, made out of your Spirit. Your Word formed life within them. You spoke words of life in the atmosphere, and both heaven and earth responded.

Father, when you created:
- You said, "Let there be light," and there was light.

KINGDOM INTERCESSION

- You said, "Let there be a firmament in the midst of the waters," and it was so.

Father, when you commanded:
- You said, "Let the waters bring forth moving creatures and fowls," and the waters obeyed.
- You said, "Let the earth bring forth grass and yielding seed," and the earth obeyed.
- You said, "Let the earth bring forth the living creature after its kind," and the earth obeyed.

Father, when you designed:
- You said, "Let us make man in our image, after our likeness, and let them have dominion over … all the earth," and man was created and uniquely designed.
- You formed man of the dust of the ground, breathed into his nostrils the breath of life, and man became a living soul.

You are the creator of all things, the giver of life. Your words are so powerful that everything in the universe adheres to your voice. You created us to speak into the atmosphere, and our prayers are words of power.

Father,
- let there be light in our prayers to bring forth life in the lives of your people;
- let there be a holy conversion between you and your people to restore us in your sight;
- let there be blessings upon our land and let milk and honey flow from it like never before;

- let there be an open gate in your spiritual garden for your beloved to enter in and eat the fruits at your table;
- let there be provisions made for widows, orphans, and the poor;
- let there be wisdom and knowledge imparted into your people to overthrow ignorance;
- let there be more prophetic visions to enlighten your prophets, apostles, and evangelists;
- let there be a watchman on the wall to sound the alarm in prayers when evil is present;
- let there be renewal of marriage vows in the land of your people;
- let there be no fornication among the unmarried, both adults and the youth;
- let there be pure worship of spirit and truth in your churches, temples, and tabernacles;
- let there be freedom in all the nations to worship and acknowledge you as the true and living God;
- let there be dew and rain upon the earth to bring forth the harvest in due season;
- let there be an anointing of your Spirit in the earth to break the yokes of Satan;
- let there be a kingdom mind-set among on your people to bring forth wisdom and the understanding of heavenly things;
- let there be an inner chamber of prayer in the heart of your people so they will seek you in that secret place;
- let there be peace in Jerusalem always and forever; and
- let there be kingdom intercession.

In Jesus' name we pray. Amen.

CHAPTER 6

Holy Communion

Communion with God is holy, and that is why our prayers have significant meaning and purpose. Engaging in sincere prayer and intercession creates an atmosphere for Holy Communion because of the intimacy and spiritual unity. The word *commune* means to communicate intimately.[4] The Scriptures show us in many instances how we are to commune or be in spiritual union with God through the working of the Holy Spirit.

In the beginning, God established the model for Holy Communion with his people. He communed with Adam and Eve constantly. This was a way of life for them. We can only imagine the conversations they had with the Creator of heaven and earth. The garden had to be the perfect place to have communion with God. I believe that no stress, hurt, pain, or even tears existed in the garden of Eden. The Scriptures do not mention any crying or distress until after the fall. Before that time there was no sin, and everything should have been

---

[4] *Merriam-Webster's Collegiate Dictionary.* Springfield, Massachusetts, U.S.A.: Merriam-Webster, Incorporated, 2012.

full of love, peace, abundance, and overwhelming joy. God had given them everything they needed, and they were one in him.

Only when we break away from communion with God are we faced with temptation and adversity. When we commune with the Father, our attitudes and mind-sets change. As an effort to have a lifestyle of communion with the Father, we should practice renewing our minds daily so our thoughts and deeds can be governed by God. Communion with God, by way of the Holy Spirit, helps bring to our memories his greatness and how much he loves us. Communing with him also strengthens as we become deeply planted like trees. For these reasons, sincere intercession is essential.

Many refer to the term *Holy Communion* as a participation of worship by partaking in the eating of the bread and wine, as Jesus did during the Last Supper. This was and still is a prophetic activity that Jesus performed. The point is that any communion with God should be heartfelt and holy because *he* is holy. In the following passage, the communion referenced at the Last Supper was the introduction to a new life.

> Now as they were eating, Jesus took bread, and after blessing it broke it and gave it to the disciples, and said, "Take, eat; this is my body." And he took a cup, and when he had given thanks he gave it to them, saying, "Drink of it, all of you, for this is my blood of the covenant, which is poured out for many for the forgiveness of sins.
>
> —Matthew 26:26–28

As mentioned earlier, this was a prophetic activity and sacred ritual Jesus used to represent the "bread as His Body (flesh) and the wine as His Blood (covenant)." Prophetic activity is described as "a series of spiritual actions and ministry deeds performed by the prophet." "Prophetic activity conducts the works of the Lord as they constitute the purposes of God for those to whom the prophet is sent."[5]

In the book of Matthew, we read that Jesus first blessed and broke the bread and then gave each a portion. To me, this means we all share in the body of Jesus; he was broken for all of us who partake in communion with him. Then he took the cup of wine and blessed it and gave it to them to drink as it represented the blood that was shed for forgiveness of our sins.

The atmosphere in the room had to be conducive to the Holy Spirit for Jesus to implement this sacrifice. The communion was already in process. Without being there physically, we could still perceive the prophetic anointing that took place in that room as Jesus spoke these words and used his body to perform the ritual. John 6:52 says, "The Jews therefore quarreled among themselves, saying, How can this man give us his flesh to eat?" Many today still are not able to receive this doctrine. This is why we need intimate prayer time so the Spirit of truth can reveal these things to us.

Now the book of John takes us a step deeper. In his prophetic style, John clearly tells us in Chapter 6 that Jesus is the bread of life from heaven, and if we believe on him, we will never thirst. He is the bread that came down from heaven. This teaches us an increased level of understanding of the spiritual meaning of the broken bread and how we partake in it when we commune with him. Jesus was sent from heaven in the form of a physical body that was broken as the ultimate sacrifice for our sins.

---

[5] Price, Paula. *The Prophet's Dictionary, Revised and Expanded Edition*. ed. New Kensington, PA: Whitaker House, 2006.

> Then Jesus said unto them, Verily, verily, I say unto you, Moses gave you not that bread from heaven; but my Father giveth you the true bread from heaven. For the bread of God is he which cometh down from heaven, and giveth life unto the world. Then said they unto him, Lord, evermore give us this bread. And Jesus said unto them, I am the bread of life: he that cometh to me shall never hunger; and he that believeth on me shall never thirst.
>
> —John 6:32–35

The apostle John was definitely one who communed with God. All the disciples were used greatly, but I feel that John had a deeper anointing. In his books, you will find him to be exceptionally prophetic. Furthermore, God used him to write the book of Revelation. John tells us that the Word was made flesh and dwelled among us. This, too, represents Jesus as being sent from heaven and his physical body having significant meaning. He is the living Word and the bread of life, and as we abide in him and he in us, we can have eternal life. The Word of God is full of life. When we eat and drink of it, we will not hunger or thirst. Our Father in heaven sent Jesus to earth not only to die for our sins so we could be forgiven but also to feed us so we could become one in Christ.

> In the beginning was the Word, and the Word was with God, and the Word was God. The same was in the beginning with God.
>
> —John 1:1–2

> And the Word was made flesh, and dwelt among us, (and we beheld his glory, the glory as of the only begotten of the Father,) full of grace and truth.
> —John 1:14

> That whosoever believeth in him should not perish, but have eternal life.
> —John 3:15

Our prayers should be that everyone believes on the Son of God and his purpose. By faith, we eat of his body and drink of his blood in Holy Communion in gratitude for Christ's works. We are made partakers of Christ as we hold onto our beliefs until the end according to Hebrews 3:14.

Being in Christ is a wonderful place to be. David makes a powerful statement when he says, "O taste and see that the LORD is good: blessed is the man that trusteth in him" (Psalm 34:8). This holds true for the believer. We have to trust that the Word of God is true, pure, and infallible. Once you get a taste the Word, you will always come back for more. When God prepares the table for his people, there is nothing comparable or more fulfilling.

> For we are made partakers of Christ, if we hold the beginning of our confidence steadfast unto the end.
> —Hebrews 3:14

> For it is impossible for those who were once enlightened, and have tasted of the heavenly gift, and were made partakers of the Holy Ghost, And have

tasted the good word of God, and the powers of the world to come.

—Hebrews 6:4–5

Some may wonder how all of these things tie together, but that's the glory in God. Understanding comes softly. Jesus is an extraordinary example for us. What he accomplished through the cross is greater than anything this world could ever do because of its universal impact on all mankind. After we lost our access to the Tree of Life after the fall of Adam, Jesus restored us through his own death. This was indeed the greatest thing that ever happened to us. Any impact on mankind occurs under the surveillance and oversight of God because we are his unique creation and design.

Believing in the Word of God makes life easy; unbelief makes life harder. Doubt and unbelief are negatives that take away from your spiritual growth. They are a constant drawback because God created us to believe in him. He made us in his image (Gen 1:27), and that image is the reflection of Christ. How can we not believe? When we simply believe what his Word says, not only are we increasing our spiritual growth but we are also honoring the Son and therefore the Father. "That all men should honour the Son, even as they honour the Father. He that honoureth not the Son honoureth not the Father which hath sent him" (John 5:23).

Holy Communion

> **Spiritual Thoughts**
>
> When we partake in the body of Christ, by faith we commune with each part of the body:
>
> - his head, which represents kingship
> - his legs that walked on earth for us
> - his hands that he laid on the sick and they were healed
> - his feet that were prepared with the gospel of peace
> - his eyes that saw into eternity
> - his mouth that preached the kingdom of God
>
> All of these represent the body of Christ. When we take communion with bread and wine, we should view it as eating each part of his body and truly drinking his blood to represent the everlasting covenant.
>
> Keep in mind that this is a sacred and intimate observance that signifies our beliefs and relationships with God.

Kingdom Intercession

Our Father in heaven, how boundless is your love for us. Words could never express your greatness. You created us with the perfect design with precise specifications and plans for mankind. Satan and even man may try to replicate your works, but your wisdom is so vast and endless, they could never come close to your original imprint. Who knows the number of hairs on our heads but you? Who decides when we are born and when we die? Who can hear our heartbeats or know our every breaths but you?

Father, you sent your Son to the earth in the flesh as an example of what the image you made us in looks like. You gave us bodies that were functional by design, free from infirmities, with internal organs that were perfectly arranged in every dimension. We were created to rule over everything on the earth. We have predetermined instructions that are laid out in the blueprint of your Holy Word.

Thank you for the privilege of communion with you through your Son. As we partake in his broken body, we reverence what he did for us through the cross, the resurrection, and the coming of the Holy Spirit. Father, we commune and partake in every part of Jesus' body:

Father,
- we pray that our legs will be strengthened to stand in the midst of adversity as Jesus did;
- we pray that we will remain the head, which represents the restored authority you have given us in the earth through Jesus;
- we pray that our hands will be instruments for healing as we lay our hands on the sick as Jesus did;
- we pray that we will walk in peace, and that wherever the soles of our feet tread shall be ours in the name of Jesus;
- we pray for the vision to see into the inner chambers of our spirits as Jesus did;
- we pray that the words of Jesus shall be on our lips forever;
- we pray for ears like Jesus to hear and discern in the spirit;
- we plead the blood of Jesus over every area of our lives;
- we thank you that every spoken word of Christ Jesus is sealed by the blood of Jesus;
- we thank you for sending the bread of heaven to give us life;

- we thank you for the blood that flows on every mountain and through every valley;
- we thank you for washing us clean with the blood of Jesus; and
- we thank you for the everlasting covenant through the blood of Jesus.

Father, your Word tells us in John 16:23 that whatsoever we ask the Father in Jesus' name he will give to us. Thank you for allowing us to commune with you through worship, praise, and, most of all, prayer and intercession. We are forever grateful for your presence. We yearn for intimacy with you as we partake in Holy Communion. In Jesus' name we pray!

CHAPTER 7

From the Heart of an Intercessor

The heart of an intercessor has a deep love and passion for prayer, and praying becomes an intercessor's heartbeat and lifestyle. A devoted intercessor will yearn for the presence of God to allow the Holy Spirit to make intercession through prayer. Fervent intercession is communing with God spirit to spirit. This communion opens the door for the Spirit of God to operate freely within you through prayer to manifest his will on earth.

Passionate prayer transformed my life from a sinner to an intercessor. He called me out of darkness into his marvelous light. When I truly repented and confessed Christ as Lord and Savior over my life, God began to work in me. He met me right where I was in my spiritual walk and drew me closer to him. As I read and studied the Bible, God added to my life, and I knew that this change was forever. Prayer was the gateway, and I am forever grateful.

My prayer life went from zero to ten in the first six months. I still recall not knowing what to say to God. I kept saying, "He is the creator of heaven and earth, and he did things that no man could ever do." He divided the light from the darkness, divided the waters, and created the days, to name a few. God commanded the sun to stay in the sky in the beginning of time, and it remains there today. I would ask, "What do I say to the one who is all in everything?" He is all-knowing, all-powerful, all-seeing, all-in-all. Nevertheless, he placed the words in my heart, and I begin to speak to him. Eventually, my prayers grew from a few sentences to an entire conversation with the Father in heaven.

As our prayer conversations increased, I grew and matured. Eventually, the things I desired began to dissolve, and my life was changed. The more I talked to God, the more he transformed me.

My prayer life was being developed for a greater purpose. The Holy Spirit began leading me into a deeper level of intercession. At that time, I did not fully understand the impact of intercession. I would pray for others, but mostly those in my immediate circle. However, in my prayer time with God, he began giving me images of people, places, and even colors. As God showed me these things, the Holy Spirit led me into a deeper study of the Scriptures for clarity and understanding of what he was revealing through prayer.

The more I read the Bible, the more I could see the people God was showing me in prayer, as they had some of the same characteristics, styles, and habits of those depicted in the Bible. I was amazed at how the Word was jumping off the pages and coming to life. This was a blessing because my former reasoning believed that the Bible was history driven, not future driven, meaning that the testimonies in the Bible were only relevant to days of old. I thank God that the stronghold of deception was lifted from my thinking.

My prayer experience guided me into seeing from a spiritual perspective. Our eyes are one of the most unique organs of the human body because it is the organ that gives us our vision. They allow us to see in the natural as well as the spiritual. Our vision is vital to God and to us. Satan will attack our vision whenever opportunities arise. He is the author of deception, and his goal is to alter our vision and keep us blind so we cannot see him operating in our lives.

Prayer can open our eyes to God's vision and purpose for our lives. The more I prayed the more my vision of life changed. It is amazing how much I missed when I was blinded to the truth. Satan does not want us to pray because he does not want us to see; he wants us to remain spiritually blind. He knows if we pray we will see and believe more of the things of God. In 2 Corinthians 4:4, the apostle Paul talks about spiritual blindness, and that the god of this world (Satan) has blinded the minds of unbelievers to keep them from seeing the light of the gospel.

In some cases, people do not pray because they do not believe that prayer really changes things. If everyone truly believed in the power of prayer, they would pray at all costs. How often do we desire some change either in our lives or the lives of others? Then why not pray and ask the one who can make it possible? Why do we just accept the world's deception? The truth is the light, and the light is that God does answer prayer. I am a sold-out witness for the power of prayer.

God has answered many of my prayers and petitions. I can recall praying for a family member who was heavily under the influence of drugs. I watched the abuse impact her entire life. Drug abuse is a spiritual stronghold and the work of the Enemy. I believe that we must learn the tactics of Satan so we can know what to pray for.

At first, I asked God to protect and keep her. Then I started asking him to stop her from using drugs. Other family members were praying as well, but the condition was not changing. Then I began crying out to God in five a.m. prayer, asking him to tell me what needed to be done so she could be delivered from drugs. The Holy Spirit led me into the Word and revealed to me that she was dealing with a stronghold. Second Corinthians 10:3–5 says,

> For though we walk in the flesh, we do not war after the flesh: (For the weapons of our warfare are not carnal, but mighty through God to the pulling down of strongholds ;) Casting down imaginations, and every high thing that exalteth itself against the knowledge of God, and bringing into captivity every thought to the obedience of Christ.

The adversary was altering her reasoning to think contrary to the truth.

Drugs are one of many methods the Enemy uses to create strongholds. In most cases of demonic works, deception and lies are typically the foundation. Our targeted prayers can tear down strongholds by praying and confessing what the Word says. In Matthew 12:29 and Mark 3:27, Jesus uses the parable about first binding the strong man (Satan) before entering his house to spoil his goods. Here, the goods or possessions are those beings that carry out the works of Satan. Jesus and his disciples spoke the Scriptures over circumstances to drive out demonic forces. We have that same authority through the resurrected Jesus to bind Satan and his works to free those in captivity. The good news is that one day Satan will be bound forever!

Some nights God would wake me in the midnight hour to pray. In those times, I believed she was in the Enemy's camp, using drugs. I rose from bed and moved to the floor to engage in passionate prayer. I remember reaching out and grabbing in the atmosphere as if I was literally pulling her out of that dark place. The more I prayed, the more I could see her deliverance.

My prayers became very specific as I spoke the Word of God over her life, making declarations and proclaiming what the Word says. I prayed positive words like "I proclaim that she shall live and not die," "Father, give her strength to resist temptation so it will flee," "Let her believe in her heart what is true, pure, honest and just," "Father, call her out of darkness into your marvelous light," "Deliver and set her free in her mind, body, and spirit from the works of the Enemy," and "God, you did not give her a spirit of fear but of love, peace, and a sound mind." Also I asked God to remove the taste of drugs from her lips, and to not to let her get high when she attempted to use drugs.

While still praying, I was led to pray for others just as passionately. I prayed for anyone who may have been experiencing the same stronghold, regardless of personal relation. If I knew the names, I called them out, and if not, I called out generic names of men and women in cities, states, and other parts of the country. I prayed for those and their families who were impacted by the stronghold of drug abuse.

Not long after the process of change began, I saw God changing the situation in my family. God answered our prayers, and my sister was delivered from her addiction to crack cocaine. Now she reads the Bible and attends Bible study regularly. But most of all, she is developing her prayer life. We give God the glory and praise for what he is still doing in her life. This is only one of countless testimonies.

The point of the prayers was to include the multitude whether I knew them or not. We need to pray for one another regardless of the situation. Jesus was concerned about all of us, which is why he came, and we should adopt that same concern. If we truly are about our Father's business, we would pray for and love others more.

The Heart of the Intercessor through Scribing

As mentioned earlier, prayer has transformed my life. My Christian walk and spiritual growth has increased beyond anything I could imagine. Spiritual transformation is indeed a process, and it takes time, effort, and the leading of the Holy Spirit. Likewise, the birthing of spiritual gifts requires processing time. David was anointed king at an early age by the prophet Samuel, but first he had to go through the process of preparation before becoming the king of Israel.

When I first started writing, I would just write whatever was on my mind at that time. I wrote without any format, style, or plan and mainly jotted down my thoughts and stored the documents away. Later, I would return to the writing, and as I read it over, I would ask myself, "Did I really write this?" Sometimes I wrote things before they happened or narratives that were expounded from a particular subject. I recall writing without stopping at times, as if there were something inside of me I had to get out. This happened on many occasions.

Once I began to mature spiritually, I found myself writing more often. This time I could tell that my writing style was different, and there was a drastic change in the tone of my writing. My content had changed, and I felt like my scribing had a voice. My passion for writing was increasing, and there were times when I could stay in the Bible all day digesting the Word and then write what God was revealing to me.

Now when reading books or other literature, I closely key in on the writer's tone. All authors have their own voice in writing, which distinguishes them from other authors. When I read the journalism of Myles Munroe and Perry Stone, there is a distinct voice in their writing, no matter the subject. God has given us all a unique voice (spirit), just like our finger- or footprints. Our voices may sound alike at times, but the core is different.

My favorite author is Oswald Chambers. I love his writing. His style, content, and voice still carries the spirit of his work today. Scribing is a gift because it has a voice, and that voice comes from the spirit within. For this reason, while reading the Bible, I note the inspired author who God used to scribe his Word. Each book has a unique style and tone because of the author writing it.

I remember in Bible College having deep discussions about who wrote the book of Hebrews. Some said the apostle Paul, and some said Barnabas or Apollos. My personal opinion is that the apostle Paul may not have been the only author of Hebrews. After I read the book again with a listening ear, I noticed it had a different voice and tone than the other books that clearly identified Paul as the author. I believe we can change many things about ourselves, but the voice of our spirit remains the same.

Prayer is a major key in my writing. For me, the flow of writing is more fruitful after time spent in prayer. Meeting God early in the morning for prayer works best for me. There is something about spending the early morning hours in the presence of God. This prepares my spirit for capturing and scribing what the Spirit says to me.

In 1 Corinthians 12, the Bible talks about the spiritual gifts, and how there are diverse operations but the same God that works within them all. As the Holy Spirit unveiled my spiritual gift of prophecy, my passion for prayer increased tremendously. I believe that without a sincere prayer life, the operation of spiritual gifts may not be as fruitful.

This brings to my remembrance when a pastor once told me that I have to acknowledge my gifts so God could make room for them. For a long time, I would not publically confess my gift. I believe at times we allow people to put us in spiritual bondage that causes us to believe God will not use us. We become overly concerned about what others say about us. However, the Word tells us to not throw away our confidence, for it will be richly rewarded. The truth is, God places gifts in the most profound areas so he can get the glory.

The gift of prophecy and the office of a prophet are most scrutinized. The Bible portrays this in many of its books, and we often experience this today. Now there are false prophets as the Bible teaches us, but there are a lot of true prophets. If we map it back to the Word, there were many true prophets that God used in different capacities. All of them were different in character and operation. Some played major roles, and some were merely mentioned. Yet God used them for his purpose. Elijah, Daniel, Ezekiel, Jeremiah, and, most of all, the Samuel and Isaiah played major roles, to name a few. All of the prophets in the Bible operated under a different level of gifting but were led through the same Spirit.

One commonality they all had was scribing the spoken word. Some have their own book in the Bible, and some do not. I found it interesting that Baruch is referred to in the orthodox faith as a prophet.[6] In addition, his book is also known as one of the apocryphal

---

6   The Orthodox Church in America. "Prophet Baruch." . http://oca.org/saints/lives/2013/09/28/102745-prophet-baruch (accessed November 7, 2013).
"Baruch." In New Revised Standard Version Bible. ed. New York, NY: Oxford University Press, Inc. , 1989. .

books. According to Jeremiah 36:4, Baruch was Jeremiah's scribe. "He wrote, from the mouth of Jeremiah all the words of the Lord, which he had spoken unto him, upon a roll of a book."

The Jewish encyclopedia references something about Baruch that I found attention grabbing. The subject is about Baruch's grave being a legend. An Arabian king ordered Baruch's grave to be opened, but all who touched it fell dead. Then the king commanded the Jews to unfasten it, but they prepared themselves by fasting for three days and succeeded without any misfortune. Baruch's body was in a marble tomb and appeared as though he had just died. The king ordered his body to be moved to another place, but after pulling the tomb a small distance, the horses and camels were unable to move it any farther. Because of this, the Arabian king's doubts increased regarding the teaching of Islam, and as a result, he and his courtiers finally accepted Judaism. [7]

The prophetic anointing is powerful. Jeremiah was an anointed prophet. He and Baruch appeared to be very close, just like today when prophets tend to gather with other prophets. So I believe that if Jeremiah was hearing from God, and Baruch was scribing the spoken words, Baruch was also impacted by the anointing like Moses and Joshua, Elijah and Elisha, and Eli and Samuel. If Baruch's grave was still anointed after he died, what the Bible says about the prophet Elisha's anointed remains. Second Kings 13:21 tells us that when a dead man was being buried, they cast him into the Elisha's grave. As soon as the man's body touched the bones of Elisha, he revived and stood up. The moral of the story is that Baruch may or may not have

---

[7] "Jewish Encyclopedia-Baruch: http://www.jewishencyclopedia.com/articles/2562-baruch." *JEWISHENCYCLOPEDIA.COM.* : , 2013. . Print. Jewish Encyclopedia-Baruch: http://www.jewishencyclopedia.com/articles/2562-baruch

operated in the office of a prophet and been denied by man, but God still used him prophetically before and after he died.

I have learned not to struggle with the world's reasoning but to be free to operate in the spirit that God gave me. The truth lies within. The prophetic has multiple branches that stems from the vine. Paula Price defines a scribal prophet in *The Prophet's Dictionary* as:

> A prophet who has extraordinary writing instincts and literary insight into the word of the Lord, and is assigned by Him to engage in prophetic writing or prophecy interpretation for future generations. Usually assigned to present a collection of works to teach, enlighten, educate, and inform their contemporaries, ministers, and saints to come.[8]
>
> The book also gives details about how the prophets Nathan, Gad, and Shemaiah, as well as the major and minor prophets, are illustrations of this prophetic call.[9] Shemaiah here refers to the prophet of the Lord in the reign of King Rehoboam of Judah, and not the false prophet Shemaiah who is referenced in the book of Jeremiah.

A scribal prophet is found deep within the inner core of a person's soul. Scribal prophets transcribe spoken words and revelations in the form of writing and teaching. They minister to souls about the

---

[8] Price, Paula . The Prophet's Dictionary, Revised and Expanded Edition. ed. New Kensington, PA: Whitaker House, 2006, page 489.

[9] Price, Paula . The Prophet's Dictionary, Revised and Expanded Edition. ed. New Kensington, PA: Whitaker House, 2006, page 230, 510

kingdom of God. Their journalism is sincere, sacred, and has a kingdom purpose.

Being a scribal prophet involves more than just writing; it is keeping a spiritual vision open by meditating on the Word of God, listening for his voice, diligently praying, and keeping a pure heart so God can use him or her to deliver his messages. In today's world, there are different variations of prophetic works, such as nonfiction books, poetry, screenplays, and even prophetic painting, to name a few. In every case, heart and passion are demonstrated through the gift. In addition, a scribal prophet will have a strong craving for the Word of God from the intensity of the Spirit. "Then said he unto them, Therefore every scribe which is instructed unto the kingdom of heaven is like unto a man that is an householder, which bringeth forth out of his treasure things new and old" (Matthew 13:52).

The heart of a scribal prophet is full of love and passion for spiritual things, which drives the kingdom purpose imparted within him or her. The prophets' assignments are centered on the things of the kingdom of God. One does not have to be an expert journalist to be a scribal prophet; however, prophetic writing should represent God's vision as prolific, profitable, creative, and, most of all, fruitful. Our God is all that and more. He is the great Creator, and his mandate for us since the beginning of time is to be fruitful and multiply. His Word is fruitful, abundant, and fertile. The intent of a scribal prophet is to transcribe what the Holy Spirit says to bring forth much fruit through revelations and interpretations.

I believe when a prophetic call has been placed on a person's life it is usually developed and birthed through dedicated prayer and fasting and seeking the face of God. Through these channels, our spiritual eyes are opened and we can receive what the Spirit is revealing. Prophetic gifting allows us to see things from a spiritual perspective versus viewing them with our natural vision. This can be frustrating when we share what we are seeing in the spirit with others because in most cases they cannot see what we do. Therefore, most prophetic people are often misunderstood and are sometimes known as loners. They can spend hours at a time by themselves in the Word or talking to God, for he is the One who really understands who they are because he created them.

Daniel is a good example of a scribal prophet. He was blessed with a prophetic gift that allowed him to understand dreams and visions. Daniel could interpret spiritual things that God revealed to him, which were mystical and unnatural to man. He let it be known to King Nebuchadnezzar and others that there is a God in heaven who reveals secrets concerning the end times. Although God granted Daniel great knowledge and wisdom, Daniel still sought their meaning. One of the visions God sent him was the angel Gabriel to explain and bring forth understanding. These prophetic visions were recorded by Daniel and made available to all of us.

Daniel had a strong passion for God and was determined to be obedient and loyal to him. Most scribal prophets are very loyal with a strong drive concerning the matters of God. When they have a burden in their spirit, it is like a flame burning that will not go out until it is released by way of writing or speaking at the appointed time. Once the burden is released, the vessel experiences emptiness because of the outpouring of their spirit.

Daniel knew how to seek the face of God by interceding for the people. In Chapter 9, we read that he set his face unto the Lord God to seek by prayer and supplications, with fasting and sackcloth and ashes, and made his confessions on behalf of the people. To love God is to love his people.

God has revealed many spiritual messages by way of dreams and visions. There are times when I experience spiritual impartations in the form of a dream, and other times, the visions come while I am awake. There are occasions when interpretation is immediate, and other times, I must wait for God to reveal their meaning. These visions and dreams have increased over time as I have matured in my walk with God. This walk has caused my spiritual vision to grow. Some things I document, and some I do not.

Everything has an appointed time. We have to be careful not to birth things prematurely. Waiting for the appointed time can be a slow process. Sometimes the wait is long, and the Enemy will try to make you believe that you misinterpreted or that the vision was not from God. I can imagine how the prophet Habakkuk must have felt. His prophecy concerning the fall of Babylon did not come to pass for sixty-six years.

The Enemy hates spiritual writers because their words come alive when they are written. Once the words are poured out of our spirits, whether in the form of writing or speaking, they are released into the atmosphere. They become seeds, and those seeds are planted in the hearts of people who hear or read and then share them. Prophetic writers are responsible for their words just as if they are spoken out of their mouths. The Bible tells us in Matthew 12:36 that we have to give an account for careless words on judgment day. This is why it is so important to me that what I write maps back to God's Word. His Word is true and does not fall to the ground. Spiritual writers keep the Enemy on guard because they reinforce God's Word, which is life and has power over the Enemy. Jesus reminded Satan when he tempted him in the wilderness of the things that are written because words have power.

At times, certain things will be revealed as you write while the spirit is being stirred within you. A scribal prophet's writing is sensitive because it is an outpouring of what God has entrusted to you. This can happen often after you have spent intimate time with God in sincere prayer and intercession. Not everyone can receive prophetic writing, whether in inspired books, the Bible, or other sacred works, for it is foolishness to them because their spiritual vision has not been opened.

> But the natural man receiveth not the things of the Spirit of God: for they are foolishness unto him: neither can he know them, because they are spiritually discerned.
> —1 Corinthians 2:14

The heart of a scribal prophet seeks and yearns for the presence of God. Intercession is the primary key of a prophetic writer's life. The apostle John spent time with God and was taken up in the Spirit while on the island of Patmos where God showed him the things to come. He then wrote the book of Revelation as the Spirit instructed. What God revealed to the apostle John in the Spirit could only be birthed in someone who had a true spiritual love relationship with the Father. John was one of many whose hearts were filled with passion for the things of our God.

The apostle John can also be portrayed as a scribal prophet who recorded what the Spirit revealed to him concerning the last days and that the righteous will be vindicated when Jesus returns. John writes that the evil and wicked will be forever destroyed and that God's people will enter into eternity. The book of Revelation is filled with prophetic messages, especially the testimony of Jesus, as it is the spirit of prophecy. This prophetic gift is not just for our forerunners of the Bible; Jesus tell us in John 14:12 that we shall do greater works. We can do this because of the resurrection and through the Helper, which is the Holy Spirit. John's prophetic writing is still carrying the gospel to the world.

> And he saith unto me, Write, Blessed are they which are called unto the marriage supper of the Lamb. And he saith unto me, These are the true sayings of God. And I fell at his feet to worship him. And he said unto me, See thou do it not: I am thy fellow servant, and of thy brethren that have the testimony of Jesus: worship God: for the testimony of Jesus is the spirit of prophecy.
> —Revelation 19:9–10

In a scribal ministry, you will learn to seek after the secret things of God and patiently wait for him to answer. Patience is a powerful fruit, and in most cases when you wait on God, the answer will strengthen your heart and increase your knowledge concerning spiritual things. Seeking wisdom and knowledge is essential for prophetic writing. Apostle Paul prayed that God would give us the spirit of wisdom and revelation in the knowledge of him. This was important so we could have understanding of the kingdom of God.

In 2010, I published a book called *Eyes of Understanding*. This book covers different areas of understanding spiritual things. The foundation was built on Ephesians 1:18, which reads, "The eyes of your understanding be enlightened; that ye may know what is the hope of his calling, and what the riches of the glory of his inheritance in the saints." Understanding allows revelation to come forth as our eyes are opened spiritually. It is imperative that we understand spiritual things, as God himself is Spirit. God wants us to be blessed in many ways, and one of those ways is to be able to "see" him working in our lives.

> Blessed are the pure in heart: for they shall see God.
> —Matthew 5:8

Most scribal prophets not only strive to remain kingdom minded, they also have an intercessory mandate on their lives. In order to see what God sees, they have love and compassion for others. Intercessors cry out on behalf of others, even those who are not in their immediate circles. Kingdom principles apply when intercessors stand in the gap for others because of the passion between them and God. To an intercessor, praying is not an option but a lifestyle. Communing with God becomes part of their daily routine, and this desire increases as they spend time with him in prayer. Intercession is absolutely necessary in this hour in which we live and is a vehicle that activates God's will on the earth. Through intercession, God will reveal people, places, and things so the scribal prophet can intercede for the will of God to prevail concerning various circumstances and situations.

The writing of scribal prophets has a heartbeat that is steadfast and anchored in kingdom things. The voice of God can speak to the heart even when the physical body is asleep, for the Spirit is still working.

Scribal prophets will seek and study the Scriptures to hear God speak through his Word. This happens because the Word is alive and full of life-driven revelations. When the beat is off, meaning when the flow of writing has been blocked or is not in alignment with what God has revealed, divine intervention may need to occur, for the kingdom of God is not in swaying or influential words, but in power. The Holy Spirit is the driver behind the wheel of spiritual scribing.

When the flow has been interrupted, the action to take may be one of the following:

- Stop and wait for the Holy Spirit to redirect you.
- Pray so the Holy Spirit can reveal the following:
  - anything within you that is not in alignment with God
  - any hindrances, i.e., thoughts or interactions that are separating you from the flow of God
- Engage in authentic worship to break up the ground.
- Pray for clarity before proceeding to write.

> For the kingdom of God is not in word, but in power.
> —1 Corinthians 4:20

One of the most important requirements for spiritual scribing is to surrender your own intellect and reasoning. As mentioned, the Holy Spirit is the source behind prophetic scribing. Guiding and revealing the truth about a matter is the main function of the Holy Spirit. The Holy Spirit is not a secret agent; he is real and available to all who receive him. God wants everyone to receive the Spirit with the same love he gave the Spirit to us. The Holy Spirit is a secret only if we hide him.

A scribal prophet is after the heart of God and holds fast that the Holy Scriptures are God-breathed words (2 Timothy 3:16). God reveals himself through his Word, which is why it is so powerful. No matter how long we study the Word, we cannot arrive at the complete knowledge of him. Our minds could never absorb the full greatness of God. The Word not only portrays his greatness but also his glory. Just the glory of God alone exceeds any appearance of light ever imagined.

In the book of Exodus, Moses asked God to show him his glory, but God told him that no man could see his face and live. However, he told Moses to stand upon a rock and God would cover Moses' face with his hand as the glory of God passed by. After God had passed by Moses, he removed his hand so Moses could only see the back of God. If God himself had to cover Moses' eyes with his hand while the glory of God passed by, what on earth could possibly measure up to that? We serve a God so amazing and brilliant that we cannot even stand in the Illumination of his glory here on earth and live. Wow!

> And it shall come to pass, while my glory passeth by, that I will put thee in a clift of the rock, and will cover thee with my hand while I pass by.
> —Exodus 33:22

Trust is a leading factor in the relationship between a scribal prophet and God. When trust is established and confirmed, the Lord will reveal his spoken words in different forms, but it is up to the scribe to record them. Surprisingly, a scribal prophet will struggle with sharing his or her writing because the spirit of fear will try to tamper with his or her confidence. This could also be a test to ensure that your loyalty is to God and your confidence is in him. Spiritual growth will allow you to move beyond spirits that hinder your confidence.

The fear of writing is an attack of the Enemy. The Word tells us in 2 Timothy 1:7 that God did not give us a spirit of fear, but of power, love, and a sound mind. This type of fear is made worse by a "fear of people and what they will say about your writing." If you know that God has given you the gift of scribing, do not let the Enemy rob you of your gift. Deliverance of people is something every Christian will face at one time or another. Like other spirits that belong to

Satan and impose themselves in your life, this fear can be broken and removed from you. The deliverance process is recorded in Romans 12:2: "And be not conformed to this world: but be ye transformed by the renewing of your mind, that ye may prove what is that good, and acceptable, and perfect, will of God."

Falling into the trap of the Enemy by rejecting your gift has consequences. There is a thin line between rejection and rebellion. Rejecting your gift or calling can cause a person to have what many call a "Jonah experience." Jonah rejected the assignment God had given him and ended up inside a whale for several days. Rejection may not necessarily place us physically inside a whale, but it could feel like it.

God gives us his gifts freely, and we should accept them no matter what the world thinks. If we allow it, the world will keep us constrained and locked in a box of its approval. However, if we are truly God's people, we should know that every gift that comes from the Father in heaven is perfect, as James 1:17 informs us. If God is leading you to write and share what he has revealed to you, all you have to do is step out on faith and let the Holy Spirit drive. Just put on your seatbelt. Writing unto God is the same as serving him. Blessings and favor come from serving him as the Scriptures below clearly enlighten us:

- Abraham served the Lord. "And [Abraham] said, My LORD, if now I have found favour in thy sight, pass not away, I pray thee, from thy servant" (Genesis 18:3).
- Samuel the Prophet served the Lord from a child. "And the child Samuel grew on, and was in favour both with the LORD, and also with men" (1 Samuel 2:26).

- Nehemiah was a servant for the king, with whom God gave him favor.

  > Then the king said unto me, For what dost thou make request? So I prayed to the God of heaven. And I said unto the king, If it please the king, and if thy servant have found favour in thy sight, that thou wouldest send me unto Judah, unto the city of my fathers' sepulchres, that I may build it. (Nehemiah 2:4–5)

- Job was granted favor by remaining faithful to God. "Thou hast granted me life and favour, and thy visitation hath preserved my spirit" (Job 10:12).
- King Solomon writes that whosoever finds God finds life and obtains favor.

  > "Blessed is the man that heareth me, watching daily at my gates, waiting at the posts of my doors. For whoso findeth me findeth life, and shall obtain favour of the LORD" (Proverbs 8:34–35).

- Mary was highly favored by God, as she was chosen to be the mother of Jesus. "And the angel said unto her, Fear not, Mary: for thou hast found favour with God" (Luke 1:30).

Spiritual vision is a vital piece in prophetic writing. Although every Christian should desire to have spiritual vision, a scribal prophet for the kingdom must have spiritual vision for clarity and accuracy to transcribe with understanding.

From the Heart of an Intercessor

The Bible is complete, and today's prophetic writing does not change anything that was written. Yet scribal prophets are still inspired by God through the Holy Spirit to speak to his people to reinforce his Word and build up and edify the body of Christ. This is a spiritual gift manifested in the form of writing. Most prophetic writers operate in the Spirit with words of wisdom, knowledge, prophecy, and discernment. All of these gifts are different but are of the same Spirit, according to the following Scriptures:

> Now concerning spiritual gifts, brethren, I would not have you ignorant ... Now there are diversities of gifts, but the same Spirit. And there are differences of administrations, but the same Lord. And there are diversities of operations, but it is the same God which worketh all in all. But the manifestation of the Spirit is given to every man to profit withal. For to one is given by the Spirit the word of wisdom; to another the word of knowledge by the same Spirit; To another faith by the same Spirit; to another the gifts of healing by the same Spirit; To another the working of miracles; to another prophecy; to another discerning of spirits; to another divers kinds of tongues; to another the interpretation of tongues: But all these worketh that one and the selfsame Spirit, dividing to every man severally as he will.
>
> —1 Corinthians 12:1, 4–11

Kingdom Intercession has been written from the heart of an intercessor and scribal prophet. Luke 17:21 reminds us that the kingdom of God is within us. Likewise, 1 John 3:24 lets us know that "he that keeps his commandments dwells in him, and he in him, by the Spirit which he has given us." I believe that when we engage in fervent prayer, the Spirit is making intercession through our earthly vessels. The kingdom of God will never be in conflict with the will of God, which is why we should allow the Holy Spirit to lead us in our prayers to remain in his will. It is God's will for all of us to be earthly prayer vessels that he can use.

I have a dear sister in Christ who leads an intercessory prayer group that I pray with often. One of the quotes she closes intercessory prayer with is "The greatest tragedy is not unanswered prayer but unoffered prayer." As sons and daughters of the King of Kings, we should be offering prayer up to him daily as a reasonable service unto our Father in heaven.

CONNECT WITH THE AUTHOR

Stay connected with Rhonda for ministry products, speaking inquires, or submit prayer requests the contact information is provided below.

Rhonda Anderson
Kingdom Investments Prayer Ministry
P.O. Box 26881
Richmond, Virginia 23261
www.kipm.org/author

Prayer Requests
www.kipm.org/requestprayer

CPSIA information can be obtained at www.ICGtesting.com
Printed in the USA
BVOW05s1125170914

367232BV00001B/7/P